The PAX Good Behavior Game

Teacher's Guide

Dennis D. Embry, Ph.D.

Gerry Straatemeier, M.S.W.

Claire Richardson

Kim Lauger, R.N.

Janice E. Mitich

HAZELDEN

Property of
Portland Public Schools
Title I Program

Hazelden
Center City, Minnesota 55012-0176

1-800-328-9000
1-651-213-4590 (Fax)
www.hazelden.org

©2003 by PAXIS Institute
All rights reserved. Published 2003
Printed in the United States of America

No portion of this publication may be reproduced without
the written permission of the publisher

This published work is protected by copyright law. Unless a statement on the page grants permission to duplicate or permission has been obtained from the publisher, duplicating all or part of this work by any means is an illegal act. Unauthorized copying of this material violates the rights of the publisher and is directly contrary to the principles of honesty, respect, and dignity toward others, which are the foundation of Hazelden's and many of its customers' reputations and success.

To request permission, write to Permissions Coordinator, Hazelden, P.O. Box 176, Center City, MN 55012-0176. To purchase additional copies of this publication, call 1-800-328-9000 or 1-651-213-4000.

ISBN: 1-59285-062-6

Design and typesetting by Kinne Design
Cover art and illustrations by Patrice Barton

WHAT IS THE PURPOSE OF THIS TEACHER'S GUIDE?

The purpose of this Teacher's Guide is to give you in-depth information about how to play the **PAX Good Behavior Game** and background on the science and history of the game. If you want to get started quickly, plan to first use the Quick Start Guide (included in the PAX Game Kit). Then, once you have the hang of the game, read through this Teacher's Guide for more great **PAX Good Behavior Game** ideas.

IN DEDICATION

This guide is dedicated to the brilliant scientists who first actualized the promise of the original *Good Behavior Game*—Drs. Harriet Barrish, Muriel Saunders, and Mont Wolf. They created the game in 1969 at the University of Kansas, Department of Human and Family Life, after having observed an early version of its use by some unknown but honored teacher. This guide is also dedicated to the late Dr. Donald M. Baer who co-founded the science of applied behavior analysis with Dr. Montrose Wolf and Dr. Todd Risley, with the earnest desire to use the very best science to improve the human condition by finding ways to change our own frail behaviors.

The *Good Behavior Game* embodies the tenet of St. Francis of Assisi, "From small beginnings come greater goods." The change in daily behavior wrought by the game changes a child, a classroom, a family, and then a school, a community, and ultimately untold lives. As a doctoral student with Drs. Baer, Wolf, and Risley, I was able to see the immediate benefits of the *Good Behavior Game* and related strategies during their early scientific testing.

It was not until the publication of the large, randomized control studies with longitudinal follow-up that the true, long-term effects of the game were known near the close of 2000 (about forty years after the game's invention). Thanks to the longitudinal studies by Drs. Sheppard Kellam, Nicholas Ialongo, James Anthony, and others in the United States and Pol A. C. Van Lier in the Netherlands, we know that the *Good Behavior Game* can reduce the symptoms of attention deficit–hyperactivity disorder, oppositional defiant disorder, and conduct disorders, as well as lowering juvenile delinquency and substance abuse—and increasing precious time for learning. All of these benefits from some very simple, daily habits used in an elementary school classroom!

Subsequently—in the spirit of Baer, Wolf, and Risley—trials were conducted in approximately three hundred classrooms to ascertain how the simple gifts of the *Good Behavior Game* (now available in this commercial version called the *PAX Good Behavior Game*) might be accessible to all, putting the best science into common practice, for the good of all children. PAX—productivity, peace, health, and happiness—happens when children and teachers play the *Good Behavior Game*.

— Dennis D. Embry, Ph.D., President/CEO, PAXIS Institute

TOOTLE NOTES FOR THE *PAX GOOD BEHAVIOR GAME*

"Dr. Dennis Embry and the PAXIS Institute have worked hard to bring the best science to useful practice that every teacher could use."

— Nick Ialongo, Ph.D.; associate professor, Bloomberg School of Public Health, Johns Hopkins University; evaluator of the original *Good Behavior Game*

"Every elementary school classroom should have the PAX Good Behavior Game. *It is a powerful, respectful way of helping to turn around the lives of difficult children."*

— Howard Glasser, M.A., author of *Transforming the Difficult Child: The Nurtured Heart Approach*

"This PAX Good Behavior Game *makes a science-based approach accessible, fun, and useful to teachers. Dr. Dennis Embry has created one of the most proven classroom-management tools that is extremely respectful of children and teachers."*

— Lynn McDonald, M.S.W., Ph.D.; FAST (Families and Schools Together) program founder; senior scientist, Wisconsin Center for Education Research, School of Education, University of Wisconsin-Madison

"The PAX Good Behavior Game is one of the most powerful yet simple approaches to creating a supportive environment for successful student behavior."

— Dr. Anthony Biglan, Ph.D., senior scientist, Oregon Research Institute

"With the PAX Good Behavior Game, *Dr. Dennis Embry has brought to life the idea of a low-cost, yet powerful, behavioral vaccine for behavioral problems in children."*

— Ron Prinz, Ph.D., Carolina distinguished professor, Psychology Department, University of South Carolina

CONTENTS

Chapter 1: **Welcome to the *PAX Good Behavior Game*** 1

Chapter 2: **Implementing the *PAX Good Behavior Game*** 11

Chapter 3: **Addressing the Special Needs of Children** 65

Chapter 4: **Continuing Your *PAX Good Behavior Game* Efforts** 73

Chapter 5: **Evaluating the Impact of the *PAX Good Behavior Game*** 79

Appendixes

   Appendix A: ***PAX Good Behavior Game* Glossary,** 83

   Appendix B: ***PAX Good Behavior Game* Forms and Tools,** 89

   Appendix C: **"My Wonderful PAX School" Story,** 119

   Appendix D: **Meeting Federal, State, and Other Mandates,** 129

   Appendix E: ***PAX Good Behavior Game* Evaluation Tools,** 135

Notes 143

Chapter One

Welcome to the PAX Good Behavior Game

Congratulations on using the **PAX Good Behavior Game** (or PAX Game for short) in your classroom. The game will help better your classroom, the lives of your students, and your entire school. With this proven, best practice, you'll better your own life, too!

The PAX Game is based on a game that was developed about forty years ago by a classroom teacher. Since then numerous research studies have shown that this game decreases discipline problems, increases student learning, and even reduces tobacco, alcohol, and other drug use, aggression, and other delinquent behaviors later in life. More information on the research behind the game is available at the PAX Game Web site: www.hazelden.org/paxgoodbehaviorgame.

> **PAX** is a Latin word that means people have productivity and peace, and they are happy and healthy. Something we all want in our schools!

Who Can Play the PAX Game?

This version of the PAX Game is geared to children in grades K–6. The game can be used effectively with almost all students in this age group, including those with special needs. The game can also be adapted for use with preschool-age children (see pages 65–67 in this guide) and secondary-age children.

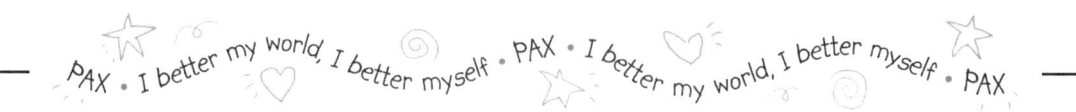

Thank you for purchasing the *PAX Good Behavior Game*.

Restock or enhance your game with these components:

- **Schoolwide Implementation Guide**
  This manual shows how to make your school a PAX school. It gets all site leaders onboard—staff, student representatives, families, and community stakeholders—for easy implementation of this best practices and research-based game. *Order No. 2117*

- **Video**
  An excellent tool to help teachers implement the *PAX Good Behavior Game*. *Order No. 7378*

- **Home Notes**
  Colorful, mailable postcards get parents interested and involved in the PAX Game while letting them know about their child's positive behavior. Sold in packs of 120 (4 designs, 30 of each design). *Order No. 2124*

- **Reward stickers**
  Make sure you have plenty on hand! Refill orders available in quantities of 60 (10 of each design). *Order No. 2125*

- **Team Wristbands**
  A fun, easy way to reinforce team spirit and belonging. Sturdy acrylic with snap closure. Pack includes 32 wristbands in 4 colors, 8 wristbands in each color. *Order No. 2126*

- **Training**
  Ideal for schoolwide or multiclass implementation, these training seminars show site leaders how to play the game and how to adapt it to their specific site needs. On-site or regional seminars available.

To place an order or for training information, call us today at 1-800-328-9000. Or visit our Web site at www.hazelden.org/bookplace.

What Is the PAX Game?

The PAX Game is a daily *practice,* NOT a curriculum, used by a teacher during regular classroom instruction. Three times a day the teacher sets a timer for three to five minutes up to thirty to sixty minutes, depending on the students' skill level, age, and experience.

During this time, the teacher matter-of-factly notes any disruptions (Spleems) that interfere with the goal of having a wonderful classroom where positive learning takes place (PAX). When the timer rings, any team with three or fewer Spleems wins that PAX Game. Winners earn a small prize either immediately (when just learning) or at the end of the day or week (as game skills increase).

Children find the game exciting and teachers find it to be a powerful tool to decrease classroom disruptions and increase the amount of engaged learning that occurs. Everybody wins with the PAX Game!

Adding PAX Cues

Once the basic game is mastered, the teacher can add PAX Cues. These are different nonverbal strategies (PAX Quiet, PAX Hands, PAX Voices, stop-and-go signs, PAX Stix, and Beat the Timer). Used on a daily basis, they help to reduce disruptions, downtime, and distress, while gaining many minutes of additional instruction during the day.

Adding PAX Tootles

Tootles are the opposite of tattles. Tootles are written notes or verbal messages created by students, school staff, and family adults and are intended to acknowledge, honor, and increase the positive behaviors of others on a daily basis.

All together, the components that form the
***PAX Good Behavior Game* are simple yet powerful daily practices.**

Why Use the PAX Game?

Imagine if teachers like you had:

- A 50 percent to 90 percent reduction in disruptive or disorderly behaviors in your classroom, hallways, and other public spaces.

- Twenty-five percent MORE time for teaching and learning, amounting to the equivalent of another month or more of school for "free."

- A 20 percent to 50 percent increase in the number of children being fully engaged in learning.

- A 10 percent to 30 percent reduction in the need for special education services, while providing real support for special-needs children in your classrooms.

- A 30 percent to 60 percent reduction in referrals, suspensions, or expulsions.

- A 50 percent reduction in the use of tobacco or other drugs over a child's lifetime so that the next generation of children comes to school with fewer problems.

- A major reduction in your own stress level.

- A major improvement in family support for your classroom.

- A way to meet state and national education mandates, such as No Child Left Behind and Safe and Drug-Free Schools, without losing academic learning time (see appendix D for more information about how the PAX Game will help you meet these mandates).

All these outcomes are possible with the PAX Game!

**If these benefits sound good,
then playing the PAX Game is for you!**

This guide will walk you through the process of making your classroom even more wonderful by playing this best-practice, scientifically proven, and real-world-tested *PAX Good Behavior Game*. A wonderful world of PAX awaits you!

The Power of the PAX Game

A state with one of the highest rates of substance abuse is bound to have many children show up at school with special needs. A town that contains the men's state prison is bound to have more than its share of children who come to school with many barriers to academic success. . . .

> This was the state, town, and school of Nancy Doty—one of Wyoming's award-winning elementary school teachers. When the Governor's Office funded a pilot project of the *PAX Good Behavior Game* at her school, Mrs. Doty enthusiastically joined in and quickly became a champion in the process of reclaiming Wyoming for the future of children.
>
> During the first days of using the PAX Game, Mrs. Doty immediately saw a difference in her class. The children were more attentive, there were fewer disruptions or distractions, and the children seemed to be learning more.
>
> When the Wyoming Education Association did a television story about her classroom's use of the *PAX Good Behavior Game,* Mrs. Doty explained, "If a child is exposed to this program consistently for as little as one year, you will see academics improve and risk factors in children's lives reduced." What Mrs. Doty was too modest to say in front of the TV cameras was that her class, which included eight special education children, now had among the highest test scores in the district.

What Is the Research behind the PAX Game?

The strategies used in the PAX Game have a great deal of science behind them. That science is briefly reviewed here so that you'll know how the PAX Game meets various federal and state mandates for research-based strategies. If you would like to read more about this research, consult the references listed at the end of this guide, and visit the PAX Game Web site at www.hazelden.org/paxgoodbehaviorgame.

The PAX Game has forty years of research behind it.
The PAX Good Behavior Game is the culmination of forty years of scientific study by many investigators. Approximately twenty published studies have shown that the game results in reduced classroom disruptions, fewer symptoms of inattention and impulsivity, reduced aggression, more time for teaching and learning, reduced need for special education or mental health services (for some students), as well as reduced alcohol, tobacco, and other drug use later in life. The game has also been shown to strengthen children's ability to consciously inhibit negative behavior and attend to learning. At this writing, no other simple strategy that an individual teacher can do has so many proven scientific results.

The PAX Game is not just *one* intervention. Rather, it is composed of many scientifically proven interventions. So, when this guide says, "Play a secret PAX Game once a day" or "Appoint a shy child as team captain," those suggestions are not just made up. They are recommended as the result of one or more actual classroom experiments.

PAX Cues such as Beat the Timer have been the subject of about fifteen studies, and even something as simple as the Stop Spleems and Go PAX signs have been separately studied in classrooms. Tootle Notes and similar strategies have been systematically studied for their effects on resiliency and behavior.

The PAX Game is a "best practice."

Just about everybody wants to say his or her program or approach is a "best practice." Why? Because money is at stake. Various federal mandates and funding sources require the use of best practices.

A best practice is not what somebody says is good. A best practice must not only meet the highest standards of scientific proof, it must also meet real-world "consumer-report-type" tests for ease of use, durability, and practicality.

PAXIS Institute, the creator of this commercial version of the *Good Behavior Game,* searches out and refines practices that are truly best practices. The *Good Behavior Game* is proven effective, using scientifically tested procedures that have resulted in credible findings by multiple investigators. These testing procedures have shown that the *Good Behavior Game* has a strong effect size,* works in real-world conditions, has long-term results, works for people of different cultures and backgrounds, can be combined with other procedures, and works even when it isn't used exactly as described or for the right length of time. PAXIS Institute has put those findings and related tools in a kit so that this best practice can become more commonly used.

The PAX Game is a "behavioral vaccine."

The PAX Game is a "behavioral vaccine." Like regular toothbrushing or hand washing, if played several times a day, it will dramatically reduce many short-term and long-term problems.

---

* When scientists talk about good scientific results, they increasingly use the phrase "effect size." This does not refer to statistical significance. Rather it is an objective measure of strength of a treatment, intervention, or medication. An effect is a brilliantly simple concept of dividing the mean difference between an experimental group and the control group. If a resulting effect size is 0.0, that means there was no difference between using the intervention versus not using it. If the effect size is negative, it means the intervention caused more negative outcomes than if no intervention was done. If the effect size is less than +.25, it means that the intervention might be useful but not very powerful. If the effect size is +.4 to +.7, then it's fairly powerful. If it's better than +1.00, the outcomes are extremely powerful. The PAX Game has an effect size between +.4 and +.7.

If you have ever been to the doctor for an illness, you've probably heard a message like: "For the medication to work, you need to take one tablet three times a day for ten days. If you don't, your illness may come back even worse." The doctor's instruction is about dose and fidelity. You have to take one tablet three times a day, which is the dose. Then you have to continue taking it for ten days, which is fidelity.

Behavioral vaccines have dose and fidelity requirements, too. The PAX Game needs to follow a certain dose with fidelity to achieve effects (with some flexibility). Playing the game for a few days, then stopping, or playing once a week simply won't produce the benefits you are hoping for. You need to play the game on a consistent, daily basis to see long-term results in children's behavior.

The Fidelity and Dose Checklist in appendix B on pages 91–92 summarizes the needed dose and fidelity of each part of the PAX Game to produce the best results for you and your students.

How Might the PAX Game, Cues, and Tootles Affect Children's Brain Functioning?

Did you know scientists have proven that earning a reward or recognition for achieving a goal by one's own actions produces a burst of dopamine in the brain of humans, primates, and other animals? Increasing a person's ability to inhibit (stop) negative behavior and increase (go) positive behavior creates dopamine. Behavior changes brain chemistry, and brain chemistry changes behavior. Seeing other people behave positively even changes our brain chemistry, and our behavior in turn.

Doctors and scientists know that medications such as Ritalin™ work on the dopamine circuits of the brain to reduce problem behavior. Scientists, teachers, and parents have observed that powerful behavior strategies such as those applied to the PAX Game also reduce the same behaviors as the medication. The PAX Game may not replace a child's need for medication, but it may help his or her behavior. What's more, scientists have very strong laboratory research which indicates that feedback and rewards (strategies that have been applied to the PAX Game) change dopamine levels in the brain. For example, the prestigious scientific journal *Nature* reported a study showing that the human brain releases dopamine when people "score" a win on a computer game.[1]

Children's brains are also wired to detect any perceived threats to their safety, to detect whether other people care for them, and to estimate their competence in handling situations involving peers. If they are learning, living, or playing in social environments that they *perceive* as fearful, threatening, or dangerous, their brains will release stress chemicals. These stress chemicals bind up the availability of brain chemicals such as serotonin (which regulates moods and thoughts about other people) and dopamine (a sort of stop-and-go reward molecule).

When strategies such as PAX Cues and tootles are implemented, children report more positive *perceptions* of their peers and adults. Children tend to see their world as safer and saner, and they see both adults and peers as significantly less likely to engage in threatening, angry, or mean behaviors.

Humans are wired to perceive social support, friendships, and a sense of belonging. It's necessary for survival. When people feel depressed, anxious, or afraid, the levels of serotonin in their brains go down. When people feel loved and cared for and have a sense of belonging and safety, their levels of serotonin increase. People feel happy and competent and are less likely to need immediate rewards or to use tobacco, alcohol, and other drugs.

Playing the PAX Game and using PAX Cues and Tootle Notes creates a classroom environment where children feel safe, loved, and cared for, and have a sense of belonging. As a result, achievement and morale typically improve as do measures of health and emotional well-being. Not surprisingly, kids learn more, and teachers feel less stressed.

The PAX Game, Cues, and Tootles Even Help Children from Difficult Home Situations

Some people ask, "How can any of this help children coming from really difficult home situations?" The answer is clear. The PAX Game—especially PAX Cues and tootles—helps kids live happier, healthier, and more productive and peaceful lives in spite of their home situations. In fact, one study compared children who participated in the *Good Behavior Game* versus students who got a powerful parent program that is widely considered to be a best practice. Guess what? The *Good Behavior Game* had more lasting, powerful effects.[2] That is really good news. Teachers who use the PAX Game can and do better the lives of their students, even their home lives.

CHAPTER TWO

Implementing the PAX Good Behavior Game

The PAX Game Kit contains powerful, but simple, evidence-based strategies to improve the conditions for learning in your classroom. There are basic steps you can take to implement the game. The Quick Start Guide goes through these steps quickly. More in-depth information is provided here.

Getting Started with the PAX Game in the Classroom

Please note that the PAX Game can start at anytime during the school year—fall, winter, spring, or even summer school. Remember, this is not a curriculum or program, but a behavioral vaccine that can be used while you are teaching other things.

The Classroom Implementation Flowchart (shown on page 12) outlines the basic steps in implementing the game in your classroom. Each step is described in more detail later in this chapter.

Setting Up a PAX Game Classroom Implementation Schedule

You can use the form shown on page 13 to schedule key dates for implementing the PAX Game in your classroom. Each activity is described in more detail later in this Teacher's Guide.

Note: If you are implementing the PAX Game as part of a schoolwide effort, you will be following a different schedule. Please check with your site leaders.

PAX Game Classroom Implementation Flowchart

PHASE 1 GETTING READY	PHASE 2 STARTING UP	PHASE 3 BUILDING SKILLS	PHASE 4 KEEPING IT GOING
☐ Attend a PAX Game training, if possible. ☐ Become familiar with the PAX Game. ☐ Photocopy and prepare all PAX Game forms. ☐ Establish baseline data for your class.	☐ Introduce the basic steps of the PAX Game. ☐ Play the game three times a day for three to five minutes. ☐ Introduce team roles, secret games, and a variety of prizes. ☐ *Optional:* Introduce the PAX Promise. ☐ Practice the game with special-needs students. ☐ Measure changes in student behavior.	☐ Introduce PAX Cues and Tootle Notes. ☐ Continue to play the game three times per day, increasing the game time. ☐ Rotate game jobs. ☐ Rotate teams. ☐ Introduce the Parent Booklet. ☐ Measure changes in behavior. ☐ Check the PAX Game Web site for new ideas.	☐ Increase game time to thirty to sixty minutes. ☐ Reward only daily or weekly prizes. ☐ Play the game as you move about the school. ☐ Maintain the proper dose and fidelity of the game. ☐ Measure changes in student behavior.

PAX Game Classroom Implementation Schedule

ACTIVITIES	DATE(S)
1. *Optional:* Attend a PAX Game training. Check with Hazelden Publishing for trainings in your area.	
2. Become familiar with the PAX Game. Read through the Quick Start Guide and this Teacher's Guide.	
3. Photocopy and prepare all your PAX Game forms. Directions are outlined in this Teacher's Guide.	
4. Establish baseline data on your class. Before implementation of the game, record the number of Spleems that occur in three, fifteen-minute periods.	
5. *Optional:* Administer the PAX Yesterday Survey (for grades 3–6). You may need to send a letter to parents to inform them of the survey.	
6. Introduce the basic steps of the PAX Game in one day. The steps are outlined in this guide and in the Quick Start Guide. Send Home Link Flyer 1 to parents/guardians.	
7. During the rest of the first week, introduce these new components to the game: team roles, playing secret games, the PAX Promise (optional), and a greater variety of prizes.	
8. During the second week, introduce PAX Cues. Send Home Link Flyer 2 to parents/guardians.	
9. During the third week, practice the game so it runs smoothly.	
10. During the fourth week, introduce Tootle Notes. Send Home Link Flyer 3 to parents/guardians.	
11. During the fifth and sixth weeks, send Home Link Flyer 4 to parents/guardians and introduce the Parent Booklet.	
12. During the seventh and eighth weeks, increase your PAX Game time.	
13. During the ninth through fourteenth weeks, generalize the use of the PAX Game to other activities.	
14. During the fifteenth week and beyond, make the PAX Game a habit for the children's futures.	
15. Evaluate the change in students' behavior. This should be an ongoing effort beginning about the fourth week. Send Home Link Flyer 5 to parents/guardians.	

Establishing a Baseline of Behavior

In order to show the effectiveness of the PAX Game, you will want to measure the amount of negative behavior in your classroom before implementation. Later you will measure again, showing the positive change since implementing the game.

To establish a baseline of behavior, play three secret PAX Games (secret because children do not know you are playing) one or two weeks prior to implementing the game. Count the number of disruptions, or Spleems, during these three, fifteen-minute periods and then calculate the average. This is your baseline against which you will compare future measurements. After playing the PAX Game for several weeks, the average number of Spleems should decrease. Graph this baseline data. If you can't play three secret games one or two weeks *before* implementation, play at least three secret games *during* the first week of implementation. Use these observations as your baseline.

Whether playing a secret game or regular game, be consistent in what you define as negative behavior or in what you call a Spleem. Inconsistency in this area will reduce the effectiveness of the intervention. Here are examples of Spleems:

Standard Spleems
- Arguing with a mean tone
- Blocking or stopping activity
- Blurting out
- Bothering a neighbor
- Breaking pencils
- Burping
- Doodling on desks or books
- Dropping books
- Fiddling with objects and distracting others
- Flipping papers to irritate others

- Getting others into trouble
- Grinding the pencil sharpener
- Hamming it up
- Hiding one's own or others' work
- Insulting other people
- Laughing or giggling at disruptive actions
- Leaving one's seat during inappropriate times
- Looking away so as to ignore the lesson or activities
- Making animal or other disruptive noises
- Muttering to distract others
- Not sharing materials
- Obvious dawdling
- Obvious defiance
- Prejudicial comments
- Putting down others verbally
- Refusing to do work
- Saying rude things
- Sighing, groaning, moaning, or rolling eyes
- Slamming desktops or books
- Talking out to disrupt
- Tapping pencils
- Taunting or teasing
- Whispering or note passing at inappropriate times

- Others: _____
  _____
  _____
  _____

Major "Splat" Spleems

Splat Spleems count twice as much as a normal Spleem and include the following:

- Aggression
- Destroying costly property
- Fighting and causing injury
- Hitting, pinching, or punching

For more detailed baseline data, use the Spleems Observation Form and Planned Activity Check (described in chapter 5 of this guide and found on pages 139–41).

To also obtain your students' perspective on the behavior in your classroom, you may want them to fill out the PAX Yesterday Survey (found in appendix E on page 137). This anonymous survey is appropriate for children in grades 3–6. Tally the results. Have children retake the survey after you've played the PAX Game for a month or two. You should see significant, positive changes in students' perceptions of your classroom.

Note: Check with your principal to see if there are any school policies about having children fill out surveys.

Playing the First Day

Here are the basic steps of the PAX Game, which you will introduce to students on the first day. For a more concise version of these steps, consult the Quick Start Guide.

STEP 1:
Play the Are You a PAX Leader? game with your children.

Introduce the PAX Game by having children sit on chairs in a circle. Shake hands with one student and say, "My name is _____ . What's your name?" Have the child reply.

Then say, "I'm a PAX Leader. Are you?" Have the child respond, "I'm a PAX Leader, too." Then say, "I like PAX Leaders who _____." (Fill in the blank with a positive behavior quality, such as "shares with others," "listens to the teacher," "says nice things to others.")

Ask the child to share a PAX Leader quality that he or she likes. (You may need to give younger children ideas of positive behavior qualities. Older children will enjoy the mystery of trying to figure out what a PAX Leader is on their own.)

Ask the rest of the children to stand if they, too, like this PAX Leader quality. Standing students must move to a new, open chair. Meanwhile you will sit in an open chair, leaving one child standing. Do not remove chairs; keep one chair less than the number of people.

The standing child should repeat the above process. Play the game for several rounds or until you think the children have a good understanding of what a PAX Leader is (somebody who is kind to others, does nice things, etc.). This simple game helps children begin to identify PAX Leaders, and it creates a desire to become PAX Leaders. It also engages children in the process of learning about the PAX Game.

Problem-Solving Tip

If a child adamantly does not want to play or acts too aggressively, it is not necessary to make a big deal out of it. Simply ask the child to sit outside the circle "to watch our fun." Often a child will want to rejoin after a few minutes.

Also ask the children to vote on PAX Leader qualities. For example, you could say, "How many like people who are friendly? That's what PAX Leaders are," or "How many like people who are nice to you instead of mean? I guess we're all PAX Leaders here."

STEP 2:
Read aloud the "My Wonderful PAX School" story to the children.

Read aloud the simple story of a wonderful school with your class (found in appendix C on page 119). The story sets the stage for your students to begin playing the PAX Game. As you tell the story, consider doing one of the following, based on the age of your students:

- Use puppets (paper-bag, sock, or paper-plate puppets) to tell the story.

- Read the story using different voices for the different characters.

- Use a feltboard with felt characters to tell the story.

- Have students (particularly older students) act out the story as you tell it.

- Hold up the appropriate posters or forms (found later in this guide) as you tell the story.

STEP 3:
Have students help create a vision of a wonderful school or classroom.

Before this session, create two posters using the poster templates found in appendix B on pages 93–95. Make two copies of the words *See, Hear, Feel,* and *Do.* Cut out the words and mount them on pieces of posterboard, as shown here. If possible, hang both posters on a classroom wall or door where the children can easily see them.

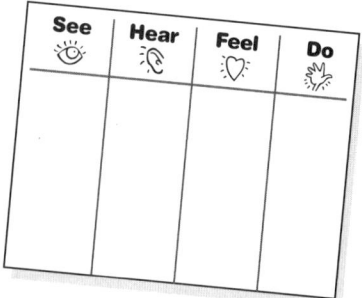

See	Hear	Feel	Do

After the story, ask the children to describe what they would see, hear, feel, and do MORE of in a wonderful school, as well as what they would see, hear, feel, and do LESS of in a wonderful school. Write their answers on the appropriate poster. *Optional:* Have the children sign the MORE poster as a way of signifying their commitment to making a wonderful classroom or school.

Added Suggestion

Once a vision for a wonderful classroom has been developed, you could repeat the process later on with other school activities or locations such as going to recess, the lunchroom, or the bathroom, or going on field trips. It would also be good to review this activity with new students who join your class during the year.

Research Note

Several studies of the PAX Game have found that when children develop a shared vision of a better world, they are more likely to internalize positive rules and behave in responsible, respectful ways, even when adults are not present. They also tend to have more "buy-in" when it comes to playing the game.

STEP 4:
Have students help develop two types of rules for the PAX Game.

From their brainstorming in step 3, the children help develop two types of rules they will live by in order to create a more wonderful classroom or school. One type of rule increases PAX, which are things that they would see, hear, feel, and do MORE of in a wonderful school or classroom. PAX examples include raising hands, using please and thank you, shaking a person's hand, and giving compliments.

> **PAX** is the peace, productivity, health, and happiness people can create.

Another type of rule decreases Spleems, which are things that the students would see, hear, feel, and do LESS of in a wonderful school or classroom. Spleem examples include tipping chairs, shuffling papers, running in the halls, groaning, or interrupting or teasing someone. For a more complete list of Spleems, see pages 14–16 in this guide.

> **SPLEEMS** get in the way of PAX or block PAX.

Now, role-play some PAX and Spleem actions for your students. Ask your students if you are acting out a "Spleem" or "PAX." Ask for a show of hands or a verbal answer. Praise correct answers. If you are concerned about a specific school or classroom rule, role-play that rule and ask the children to "judge."

You can incorporate already-existing class rules into the rules that the children develop. Write the rules to increase PAX and decrease Spleems on posterboard and post them in the classroom.

Problem-Solving Tip

Occasionally, some intermediate students may act smart or contrary during this activity as a bid for attention. Deal with any inappropriate comments very matter-of-factly, "Class, how many of you think loud burps would be a Spleem? Show me your hands. Thank you." Then move on, to avoid accidentally reinforcing the negative behavior.

Added Suggestion

If you find yourself nagging the children about these rules, try the following: once or twice a day, ask the children to predict what they will see, hear, feel, or do MORE of with some tasks as PAX Leaders. Then once or twice a day, ask the children to predict what they will see, hear, feel, and do LESS of with some tasks as PAX Leaders. For example, ask, "What would be a Spleem when walking to the library? What would be PAX when walking to the library?"

Continue to review the general rules with the children: (1) positive rules to increase PAX, and (2) rules that keep Spleems from happening. The more you have the children voice these rules, rather than saying them yourself, the better. If a class is more difficult, give weekly pop quizzes on what a PAX Leader should do in specific circumstances.

Research Note

Research shows that frequent review of these positive and negative rules helps children develop better character, especially when they believe they are playing an important role in making their world better.

STEP 5:
Divide students into three or four temporary teams.

Divide the students into three or four temporary teams with equal numbers of special-needs students on each team. Have each team wear a different color wristband (included in the PAX Game Kit) for easy identification. The wristbands are not absolutely necessary, but they are helpful in giving the children a sense of team spirit. The goal of team members is to behave in ways that will reduce the number of Spleems their team receives during each game. For the first day, use wristband colors for the names of the teams.

Important! Younger children may need help getting the wristbands on. This is a great opportunity for students to show PAX Leader behavior by helping each other. Make sure the children leave the wristbands at school so they don't get lost. If some do get lost, additional wristbands can be purchased.

Research Note
Research shows that peers often reinforce negative behavior in the classroom. The PAX Game changes all of this by motivating peers to reinforce positive PAX behavior instead.

STEP 6:
Play the first PAX Game for three to five minutes.

Make sure you play the first few games while the children are doing simple tasks, such as seatwork or book reading—nothing that requires considerable social skills or the ability to keep from being distracted by others. Preselect three prizes for the children to pick from after winning.

During the game, your job will be to circulate around the room, counting the Spleems strictly, but not with a mean spirit, words, or gestures. Here are suggestions on what to say, but adapt the wording to suit your style:

1. Announce, "We are going to play the PAX Game. I am going to be counting Spleems by each team. If your team has three, two, one, or no Spleems, you will win the game and receive a prize."

2. Mark Spleems on the Spleems Tally Sheet (found in appendix B on page 96), on a notecard that can easily be carried in one hand, or on the chalkboard next to team names. Show the class how you will record Spleems.

3. Hold up your timer and set it for three to five minutes, whatever seems appropriate. Then announce: "I am setting the timer for _____ minutes. I want you to show your best PAX behavior while we _____ (describe a simple task such as reading a book or doing math worksheets). Please start the activity."

4. Wait until the children are doing the activity, and then announce, "I'm starting the game on the count of three. . . . 1 . . . 2 . . . 3. Go, PAX Leaders!"

5. Walk around the room "tootling" about PAX, for example, "The red team is showing PAX. . . . Great PAX by the blue team."

6. Notice Spleems by teams without ANY negative emotion or sarcasm, for example, "Whoops, that chair tipping was a Spleem for the red team, Alex," or "Whispering is a Spleem for the blue team, Maria."

7. Mark the Spleems by team on the tally sheet, notecard, or chalkboard, next to the team name. Do not write the child's name who committed the Spleem.

8. Repeat this until the timer rings, and then say: "Thank you, PAX Leaders. Let's see how our teams did."

9. Check the tally sheet and say, "Let's count the Spleems by each team. Remember, if your team has three or fewer Spleems, your team wins the PAX Game." Total the Spleems for each team.

10. Have copies of the PAX Wins Scoreboard (found in appendix B on page 97) available for each team. For every team who won the game, draw a star or make a check mark on the scoreboard. You may also want to record the number of PAX Minutes won and Spleems for the game. Keep the scoreboards on a wall so the children can keep track of their team's wins.

11. Congratulate the winning teams and wish better success to the nonwinners.

12. Give each child on a winning team a prize. Prizes should be simple such as a reward sticker (provided in this kit), one minute extra recess, or two minutes listening to music. Teams that score four or more Spleems receive no prize.

13. If you are giving an immediate, timed prize, set the timer and allow the children who won the PAX Game to do the prize. Praise nonwinners for sitting in their chairs (they should not participate in the prize). Tell the children to stop when the timer rings, and then praise them for stopping.

14. Have the children continue with their lesson activities, but do not immediately replay the game.

15. Praise the class for the total number of PAX Minutes won by the winning teams during the first game. "Way to go, PAX Leaders, you already racked up ____ minutes of PAX. You are making our classroom more wonderful."

16. Keep a running total of each team's PAX Minutes won each day (for example, three PAX Wins of five minutes each equals fifteen PAX Minutes for that day). Combine these daily totals for weekly PAX Minute totals as well.

Problem-Solving Tip

Sometimes children reason that if they have "lost" a specific game, they might as well do as many Spleems as possible. To solve this, award daily or weekly wins to the teams who have the fewest Spleems in that day or week. A team may lose a game, but could ultimately win a prize by making fewer Spleems in other games. If teams tie on the daily or weekly total of Spleems, both or all can win.

☆ STEP 7:
Play two more games the first day for three to five minutes each.

Erase the tick marks on the Spleems Tally Sheet. Remind the students, "Every PAX Game begins with a clean slate." Play two more games this first day, using the same procedures. Keep playing the game during low stress or easy activities.

Problem-Solving Tip

When children lose, they may act as if they don't care about the game by saying, "I don't like this stupid prize" or other such things. Treat these comments very unemotionally by saying, "We are going to play anyway. You can sit over there while the red and yellow teams have some fun." Paradoxically, the children are telling you they really do care.

Rarely, children may attempt to ruin the prize if they lose. If you suspect this might happen, stand near the children BEFORE they can do anything, or give them a chore to do instead.

STEP 8:
Award prizes for daily PAX winners to teach delay of gratification.

During your first week of playing the game, award an immediate prize to any team that scores a PAX Win, while the other teams watch. As children get better at the game, extend the prize to the end of the day, and eventually to the end of the week.

DO NOT make the prizes long or elaborate. They should provide the brief satisfaction of having accomplished something as individuals and teams. If all the teams win, double the time for the prize—a bonus incentive for cooperation.

Delayed gratification cannot be learned by nagging, scolding, shaming, lecturing, or yelling. It is a slow process of the brain's changing, which varies depending on the child. The daily, then weekly, prizes help build this self-control muscle.

Also award a prize to the team with the fewest Spleems at the end of the day, which can be another small but different activity before going home (something as simple as being the first to leave the classroom).

STEP 9:
Send home a photocopied PAX Tootle Note and Home Link Flyer 1.

Tootling is the opposite of tattling. It is looking for the positive actions of others and then telling them and others about the actions. You are encouraged to write general Tootle Notes about your students' participation in the PAX Game during the first day. Create one Tootle Note message and photocopy it for all the students (you don't need a personalized note to every student). Send these notes home with the students, so parent(s) or guardian(s) will see them. A Tootle Note form is provided in appendix B on page 108.

Here are some example Tootle Note messages:

- "Your child's team was working really hard to not have Spleems. Great job!"
- "Students were great PAX Leaders today."

Also send home Home Link Flyer 1, which describes the PAX Game. This flyer is found in appendix B on page 110.

Tootle Notes are the opposite of tattling. They tell people about the POSITIVE actions of others.

These are the basic steps of the game that can be accomplished during your first day of play. They are simple steps, yet have been found to be very powerful in shaping the behavior of children in a positive direction.

STEP 10 (Optional):
Celebrate the students' agreeing to follow the PAX Promise and to become PAX Leaders.

Either on the first day or the next day, introduce the PAX Promise. In seeking to better the world and better themselves, the children promise to become PAX Leaders. PAX Leaders honor good actions, stop harm and blame, find trusted guides (mentors) to show them a better way, make amends, and strive to improve a little each day.

A copy of the PAX Promise is included in appendix B on page 101. Photocopy (and possibly enlarge) the promise, and then laminate it. Post it in your classroom where all the students can see it.

Optional: Have students sign the promise.

> **PAX Promise . . .**
>
> I am a PAX Leader, as you will plainly see.
> So I better my world and I better me.
>
> I honor good acts, offer help,
> and stop harm and blame.
>
> I make my amends and rejoin the game.
>
> I find trusted guides to show me a PAX way.
>
> I strive to improve, a little each day.
>
> I am proud to be a PAX Leader—at school,
> at home, in the world, and at play.

Added Suggestion

Have the children recite the promise daily or at least several times a week. They can also recite it, sing it, or perform a "rap" version of it at special events for adults, family members, or peers.

Also teach the children the PAX Motto, which is: I better my world, and I better myself. Recite the PAX Motto often as well.

Research Note

The promise of being a PAX Leader and being asked, "What would a PAX Leader do?" creates what are called Socratic, or commitment, frames. The strategy of the promise emerges also from research on helping children develop self-regulation. So-called verbal correspondence training motivates children to promise to do things and then praises them for doing what they have promised.[3]

Continuing Play during the First Week

After the first day, a class plays three games per day, moving up from three to five minutes per game to as much as an hour a game, but not more than three hours total for the whole day. It will take time to move up. Don't rush too fast. Only move up as your children show that they can win 85 percent of the time.

Research Note

Research shows that a daily dose of the game is required for the children's behavior to become a habit, since inhibiting negative behavior is actually a very difficult skill for children's brains to master.

Three announced **PAX** Games a day keep the SPLEEMS at bay!

During the rest of the first week, you can begin adding more activities to the game. Here is an overview of those activities:

IDEA 1:
Create more permanent PAX Game teams.

Assign students to more permanent PAX Game teams. Try to assign equal numbers of shy, aggressive, special education, and "normal" children to each team. Have the children pick a team name (with proper screening by the teacher). Example names include No Spleems Team, PAX Eagles, Spleems Away, PAXIDERMS, or the PAX Pros.

Added Suggestions

Rotate the teams not more than once a week and not less than once a month so children learn to collaborate with a variety of people. Award team prizes at least weekly, before new teams are formed. Plan to give longer-term prizes to the entire class, rather than individual teams.

Once your students have learned the game, consider having your whole class play as a team against another class—especially during more difficult times of the year (for example, near holidays or late spring).

Use the same teams for your cooperative learning activities, with adjustments for the mix of children.

Research Note

Through a set of ingenious studies, a number of scientists have found that peer giggles, laughter, and other forms of attention reinforce negative behavior in classrooms and are more powerful than teacher attention for good behavior.[4] In fact, peer attention for negative behavior is one of the most powerful predictors of serious trouble in a classroom. The PAX Game changes all of this by using powerful peer attention for positive behavior instead of bad behavior. The use of structured teams (as in the PAX Game) is a powerful, science-based strategy.[5]

Problem-Solving Tip

Some children seem to lie awake at night contemplating ways to mess things up. In about every third classroom, some child may decide it would be fun (meaning lots of peer attention and accidental reinforcement by adults) to sabotage a PAX Game by deliberately committing Spleems.

The creators of the PAX Game have devised and tested two strategies for dealing with this problem: PAX Game Rule 101 and PAX Game Rule 102.

- Rule 101 states that a team member may be removed from a team by a teacher for committing deliberate Spleems, also known as "Splams." The offending team member must play solo for several days up to a week. If the child's behavior improves, the teacher may reinstate him or her to a team.

- Rule 102 states that laughing, giggling, or encouraging a person who is splamming is a Spleem against one's team.

Rule 101 and Rule 102 usually need to be invoked only once or twice a year.

IDEA 2:
Play the PAX Game secretly once a day.

After playing the PAX Game for a while you may quickly notice that PAX increases and Spleems decrease when the game is being played. However, you may also notice that the good behavior declines when the game is not being played.

A simple strategy can be used to change this situation. Play the game secretly once per day (for about ten to fifteen minutes) and announce the winner(s). The children won't know when the game is being played, motivating them to behave positively at all times.

Research Note

Behavioral scientists have a technical term for these secret games. They are called *non-discriminable contingencies,* which help "generalize behavior,"[6] meaning they help children behave more positively in all situations. Businesses use the same principle with "mystery shoppers," who secretly shop at stores to evaluate customer service. Use PAX secret games to measure long-term improvement or generalization of positive behavior.

Secret **PAX** Games train the brain!

IDEA 3:
Assign students roles on their teams.

Many adults bemoan the fact that children are not responsible, reliable, or respectful. How do you teach these behaviors? Nagging and scolding children tend to produce little change in behavior.

The PAX Game resolves this problem by providing children with responsible roles on their teams, which also helps to make the game more effective. Children are praised and recognized for positively fulfilling their roles.

Here are the roles children can be assigned on each team:

- PAX Captain: This person lets his or her team know when it is time to play a PAX Game (as signaled by the teacher) and announces team wins and prizes.

- PAX Coach: This person helps team members do better at the game by using PAX Cues.

- PAX Tootler: This person reports on the positive actions of his or her team members and prompts members to write PAX Tootle Notes to each other.

- PAX Go Getter: This person collects work, passes out papers, and does other tasks for his or her team as directed by the teacher.

- PAX Reminder: This person reminds other team members of their roles, if they forget that day.

The roles are rotated from weekly up to monthly.

PAX Game Job Cards are provided in appendix B on pages 98–100. Photocopy, cut out, and laminate them. Distribute the cards to students when you assign team roles. When you rotate roles, these cards should be passed to the new team members in those roles.

Added Suggestions

Assign the role of PAX Captain to your shyer students. Playing this leadership role will help them gain confidence and improve social skills. Some long-term studies show that being in a leadership role reduces their victimization, too.

Research Note

Research shows that assigning students responsible roles in the classroom reduces negative behavior and increases academic success. School roles also contribute to the resiliency of a child coming from serious adversity, who may be showing problem behaviors such as attention deficit–hyperactivity disorder, oppositional defiant disorder, or even conduct disorders.

Anthropologically, throughout most of history—except for now in modern America—children have assumed responsible roles in daily routines to better their immediate world of home, school, and community.[7] Children need to feel that they play an important role in society and that their contributions matter.

Student responsibility roles are an "active ingredient" in some quite divergent evidence-based practices, from classwide peer tutoring to Montessori. These practices have shown long-term positive impact in randomized control studies on academic achievement and life success.[8] Also, the fact that these roles are reciprocal—that is, children take turns playing different roles—seems to be developmentally important, as one might guess.[9]

Problem-Solving Tip

Give children with "attitudes" a positive, meaningful role such as PAX Tootler. You are not rewarding bad behavior; you are intervening so that these children will be noticed by peers for doing the opposite of what they normally do—which is drawing attention to themselves in inappropriate ways.

IDEA 4:
Create different categories of prizes.

To create motivation and variety in playing the game, create different categories of prizes:

1. **Granny's Wacky Prizes:** These prizes are safe behaviors that children are normally prohibited from doing in class (such as making "arm farts" or throwing paper airplanes). Awarding these normally forbidden behaviors as prizes is a great motivator for children to participate in the PAX Game. Granny's Wacky Prizes are named after "Grandmother's Law" (also known as the "Premack Principle"), a famous finding in psychology, which states that "when you have done _____ (less desired thing), then you may do _____ (more desired thing)." A list of Granny's Wacky Prizes can be found on pages 36–38 of this guide.

2. **Kids' Prizes:** The children are empowered to come up with their own list of prizes (screened by the teacher). Extensive research suggests that people are likely to work harder for things they personally have identified as rewarding.

3. **Teacher's Prizes:** Teachers come up with their own list of challenges and prizes to motivate kids to play the game. For example, one teacher challenged the class to act positively so that every team would win every game for a week. The prize? The teacher wore her pajamas to school. Creating competition across grades or teams can be very motivating as well.

4. **Mystery Prizes:** Surprise rewards are powerful motivators to young people. For example, you might place three mystery envelopes (with prizes listed inside) on the bulletin board. Have the students choose which envelope they want to work for. Open the envelope only if the students win a certain number of PAX Games. The other envelopes, which are never opened, remain a mystery.

Added Suggestions

Brief rewards are typically quite motivating. A few minutes or even a few seconds may work. Long-reward times—ten to sixty minutes—are rarely necessary. Reserve such blocks of time for special-event-type prizes. You don't need elaborate prizes to make the game work.

Be mindful of awarding certain prizes at certain times of the day. Obviously, a high-energy reward would best be given right before recess or at the end of the day.

Research Note

The PAX Game works through the well-proven principle of pairing something positive with the completion of a responsible action. This principle—called the Law of Effect—was formally introduced in 1872. Since then, thousands of studies have demonstrated its truthfulness. One important thing to remember: a reward or reinforcement is defined by its effects, hence the Law of Effect. If something increases the frequency of a behavior, it is by definition a reward or reinforcement. Because an adult thinks something is a reward does not make it so for a child. The aim of the PAX Game is to present positive activities AFTER periods of positive behavior, which in turn make those behaviors happen more frequently.

Observe your students to find out what would be positive rewards to them. What do they naturally like to do when no rules or adults are present? Consider using these as rewards.

The following pages contain a list of Granny's Wacky Prizes that experience has shown to be very appealing to most children. You can also brainstorm ideas with other teachers or with your students. Be sure whatever prizes you choose are safe and do not embarrass or bother others.

GRANNY'S WACKY PRIZES

- Animal Noises — Students get to briefly make animal noises.

- Backwards Chair Sitting — Winning team members get to sit backwards in their chairs at their desks.

- Bad Hair Day — Students get to brush their hair funny.

- Bazillion Bubbles Shower — Using individual bottles of bubble solution and wands, students blow as many bubbles as they can in one minute.

- Being First to Bat, Being First in Line, Etc. — All winning team members are allowed to be first at something for one day.

- Burping and Arm Farts — Winning team members may VERY BRIEFLY demonstrate their most obnoxious burps, arm farts, and other disgusting noises for the rest of the class. (This is best done just before recess or dismissal and certainly not on the day of the superintendent's visit!)

- Chair Hopping — Winning team members hop in their chairs for a short time. They will tire quickly.

- Chalkboard Doodles — Children get to doodle on the chalkboard.

- Computer Time — Winning team members may use the class computer(s) during the next study time, instead of doing their work.

- Dancing Fools — Students get to jitterbug in place.

- Giggle Fest — The winning team briefly giggles and laughs while everyone else remains quiet. The teacher challenges the rest of the class to "not smile," and to definitely not make any noises.

- Giving Cuts in Line — A winning team member is allowed to give cuts in line to friends for one predetermined day.

- Grumble and Growl — Students get to grumble or growl for a brief period.

- Hangman — The winning team may play hangman for some period of time.

- Jokester — The teacher reads a book of bad kid jokes to the children. (For example, "What did King Kong call the boat filled with cocoa beans? Chocolate ships.")

- Making Faces — Teachers have all heard, "He (or she) was making faces at me," as an excuse for not being on task. Here winning team members get to make faces for a brief time.

- Nerf Toss — Students throw nerf balls at a basket, trash can, or hoop.

- Paper Airplane Toss — Everyone on the winning teams makes a paper airplane from scrap paper and then takes one turn to see who can throw his or her plane the farthest or hit a target.

- Pencil Tapping — Winning team members have two minutes to tap their pencils to their hearts' content.

- Penny-Flipping Contest — Students get to do the ancient sport of flipping pennies into containers.

- Pop Star — Children pretend to be Elvis or the Beatles and sing to some "oldie but goodie."

- Quiet Art — The winning team may do artwork instead of other work.

- Quiet Reading — Winning team members may read library books during the next study time, instead of doing their work.

- Recess Plus — The winning team receives two extra minutes of recess.

- Sit Next to Your Friend — Winning team members may choose where they sit for some period of time.

- Sit under Desks — Children get to sit under their desks.

- "The Dog Ate My Homework" Pass — The winning team is excused from completing and submitting the homework assignment for one night.

- Tic-Tac-Toe — The winning team can have a quick tic-tac-toe tournament.

- Tiptoe Tag — Students play tag indoors while tiptoeing.
- Wadded-Paper Toss — The winning team tosses wadded-up scrap paper at the trash can.
- Whispering — The winning team may briefly huddle and whisper.
- Worm Wiggle — Students get to briefly roll on the floor and wiggle.

Adding PAX Cues during the Second Week

During the second week, continue playing the PAX Game three times per day. You can probably increase the length of the games slightly during the second week, by another three to five minutes or so. You may even be able to play the game for double the time of the first week—depending on your children.

Also continue to play one secret game per day for ten to fifteen minutes each. Announce winners and make a big deal of winning a secret game. Pick easier times to play a secret game at first. Then maybe choose harder times or tasks for half of the games.

The second week is the time to introduce PAX Cues. As mentioned earlier, PAX Cues include Stop Spleems and Go PAX signs, PAX Quiet, PAX Hands, PAX Voices, Beat the Timer, and PAX Stix. Used consistently, these simple, nonverbal cues can reduce downtime and negative behavior. This section contains suggestions for teaching the cues, including short stories that show how a cue is linked to the children's vision of a more wonderful school and classroom. Home Link Flyer 2 (found in appendix B on page 112) contains information about the PAX Cues to send to your students' families.

PAX Quiet   PAX Hands

Research Note

Children make more efficient transitions and engage in less disruptive behavior when they have clear clues on how to act.[10] Comprehension of teacher verbal instructions degrades if the classroom is noisy,[11] and children or adults typically report that a great deal of negative behavior (pushing, shoving, taunting, teasing, bullying) happens in the hallways while making transitions.[12] Simple, nonverbal cues used consistently by adults can reduce downtime and negative behavior.[13]

Stop Spleems and Go PAX Signs

Highly emotional responses to children's misbehavior tend to increase their bad behavior. Why? Children learn they can "control" teacher behavior (make the teacher angry) by being bad.

In the PAX Game, Stop Spleems and Go PAX signs are placed on the students' desks (small signs) and on the walls (large signs). By tapping on these signs, teachers can give non-emotional cues to good and bad behavior while carrying on their learning activities without interruption. Several studies have found that this sort of cueing improves attention and decreases disruption. It probably reduces stress in teachers as well.

The large and small Stop Spleems and Go PAX signs are included in appendix B on pages 105–7.

Use these steps in teaching Stop Spleems and Go PAX signs:

1. Photocopy the large Stop Spleems and Go PAX signs. Post them on the walls of your classroom.

2. Photocopy the small Stop Spleems and Go PAX signs. Cut them out, fold them, and place or tape them on each student's desk.

3. Explain to the students what the two signs mean.
   - Tapping Go means "I am happy with your behavior. It is PAX behavior."
   - Tapping Stop means "I need you to adjust your behavior so it is again PAX behavior."

   During the game, tapping a stop sign on a desk can indicate a Spleem is being scored against the student's team.

4. As you teach or work with the students, simply tap on the signs and make eye contact with the children when you want to praise their PAX behavior or stop their Spleems behavior. No words are needed.

5. Award the class when you are able to go for a length of time without tapping any Stop Spleems signs.

6. *Optional:* Place the large signs on wooden stakes or poles. That way you can use these as your class moves about the building.

The stop-and-go signs are useful in situations where oral instructions would be intrusive (as when the class is preparing to leave the library or you are in the middle of giving directions) or difficult (as when you are at a distance from a group returning from recess). Use the signs for games and academic relays, when the children are moving about the classroom or walking in the hallways, or to start and stop tests.

PAX Quiet

PAX Quiet uses both a visual and auditory cue (such as a two-fingered "peace sign" and a short playing of the harmonica). Using this cue can result in transitions taking mere seconds instead of minutes, saving as much as an hour or so of time a day. The children earn recognition for quick responses, such as an elimination of a Spleem or an extra "win" on the PAX Wins Scoreboard.

Use these steps in teaching PAX Quiet:

1. When you want the class to be quiet or you want the students' attention, blow on the harmonica and hold up two fingers in a "PAX signal."* This is the signal for students to have:
   - Voices quiet
   - Hands still
   - Feet still
   - Eyes on the teacher or staff member

2. Have the children raise their hands in the "PAX signal" to show that they have heard you.

3. Individually praise three or four students for being quiet, having eyes on you, and showing the PAX Quiet signal, and then quickly acknowledge many other children with eye contact, thumbs up, and smiles. Praise the class for quick responses. Praise children each time PAX Quiet is used.

4. Give out prizes every few days for the students' quick responses to PAX Quiet.

5. A PAX Quiet sign is included in appendix B on page 102. Post the sign in your classroom as a reminder to the students.

---

* Some schools or settings may find a "feather signal" of two fingers held together or a thumbs up more culturally or politically acceptable. Something that is one-handed and easy to remember is the key.

Do the following to build the skill into a habit:

6. Praise and challenge the children to be quicker so that transitions average about five seconds instead of minutes. Use the timer or a stopwatch.

7. Children who have consistent difficulty with this task may need some "positive practice" during recess to learn to be quicker at PAX Quiet.

PAX Hands

PAX Hands are acceptable ways to hold one's hands when walking in the halls or making transitions (hands are held at one's side or behind one's back). PAX Hands reduce pushing, shoving, running, or throwing objects. Children earn recognition for demonstrating proper PAX Hands during transitions.

Use these steps in teaching PAX Hands:

1. Read aloud the PAX Hands story found on pages 43–44.

2. Draw two columns on a piece of posterboard. Label one column Harmful Hands and the other column PAX Hands.

3. Have the students tell all the ways that hands can be harmful to others or slow down the learning process (for example: pushing, shoving, or poking others). Write their responses under Harmful Hands on the poster.

4. Explain that PAX Hands never cause harm.

5. Have the students tell what to do with their hands in various situations (seated at their desks, waiting in line, walking in the hallways, etc.). Write their responses under PAX Hands on the poster.

6. Demonstrate proper PAX Hands for students.

Do the following to build the skill into a habit:

7. Praise and recognize children using PAX Hands as opposed to correcting students not using PAX Hands. Typically, the other children will join in.

8. Ask students who have problems with PAX Hands to stand near a door or at other locations to verbally prompt other students to use PAX Hands.

9. Occasionally give out wins for PAX Hands.

PAX Hands (A True Story)

Once upon a time, a school was built in a very bad neighborhood in the city. Whenever people talked about the school or neighborhood, they said, "Oh my, what a terrible place."

At school, the children walked in the halls with attitude. Some were fearful. Some were mean. Pushing, shoving, and put-downs were common. Bullying and fights happened. "Oh my," said visitors who saw it all.

The principal, who was new to the building, said, "What am I going to do? I want this school to be a more wonderful place." Fortunately, this principal knew people who studied how to make schools better places. The principal called them, and they came and showed the school how to play the PAX Game.

The students liked the new game. They made up charts of what they would see, hear, feel, and do MORE of all over the school with the PAX Game.

Some students thought they would see hands not hurting but helping. The students thought up the idea of having PAX Hands when they walked. Some did this by resting their hands gently behind them. Some put their hands at their sides. Some carried books in front of them. All these students were using PAX Hands.

As the students walked down the hall, all the adults remembered to compliment PAX Hands. "You all have PAX Hands," observed the hall monitor. The teachers made a special effort to praise PAX Hands. Suddenly, PAX Hands were everywhere in the school!

One young man decided to be a leader. He stood at the door and praised other kids for having PAX Hands. He said "PAX" to people with PAX Hands. This new job helped the boy become much more popular in school. In the past, he was often not so peaceful. People thanked him for helping. The librarian exclaimed at a staff meeting, "Oh my, have you seen what an improvement he has made? He is a real PAX Leader now."

One day, some very important visitors came to the school. The visitors strolled through the school. Everywhere they went, the visitors saw students who were calmly walking from class to class. They all were using PAX Hands.

One of the visitors exclaimed, "Oh my, what a wonderful school."

Discuss the story:

Ask the students the following questions. Call on students using PAX Stix (described on pages 50–51 of this guide), if you like.

1. What change in this true story made students happier and healthier? (Answer: PAX Hands)

2. What did the visitors say about the school at the beginning of the story? At the end of the story?

3. Do you think PAX Hands would make our classroom and school more wonderful?

4. Who can demonstrate PAX Hands to me now?

PAX Voices

PAX Voices represent different voice levels. Each voice level is appropriate for a particular situation. Adults cue children as to what level of voice they should be using and praise them for using the proper PAX Voice.

Use these steps in teaching PAX Voices:

1. Read aloud the PAX Voices story found on pages 46–48.
2. Blow the harmonica and display your "peace sign" hand signal for PAX Quiet.
3. Teach and demonstrate the different levels of PAX Voices and the hand signals for each:

PAX VOICE	HAND SIGNAL
0-Inch Voice: No talking	Make a zero with four fingers touching the thumb.
3-Inch Voice: Quiet conversational voice, barely louder than a whisper.	Hold three fingers in front of mouth.
3-Foot Voice: Normal conversational voice but not so loud that the entire class can hear.	Hold hands several feet apart.
10-Foot or Stage Voice (optional): Loud enough so everyone in the class can hear you. Use when giving a presentation.	Bring the palm of one hand from chest out with palm facing up.
30-Foot Voice: Teach but do not demonstrate. It is to be used only by adults in an emergency.	Cup hands around the mouth.

4. Practice each voice level by demonstrating the hand signals again and role-playing situations where each voice level would be used.

5. Praise the students for correctly using the voice levels.

6. Occasionally give a win or erase a Spleem for fast and appropriate use of PAX Voices.

Do the following to build the skill into a habit:

7. Reward the students for using the correct PAX Voice until they become skillful at it.

8. Use simple rewards such as a few minutes of free time or chat time, or a bonus win on the PAX Wins Scoreboard.

PAX Voices Story

"I can't think," whined one girl. "It's too noisy." A boy made a big moan. "What did you say? I couldn't hear you."

"I am FRUSSSTRATEDDDDDDD," stamped the teacher. "No one seems to follow my directions. We can't hear each other, and we are disturbing the other classes. No one seems to be listening."

Another student, Maria, spoke up, "I play music. The music teacher taught us some special words for how loud our music is supposed to be. Then we practiced, and we got praised for doing it right. Maybe we should do something like that with our words?"

"Mmm . . . ," said the teacher, "that's a good idea. I am going to think up something for tomorrow."

The next day, the teacher explained a system for helping everyone learn to use his or her voice. "I am calling this PAX Voices, because it will help us have productivity, peace, and happiness in our classroom. We'll be a lot healthier, too. We won't be yelling at each other."

The teacher explained PAX Voices, "Do you remember what Maria said about music having special words for how loud or soft something is to be played?"

"Yes," said the class.

The teacher explained. "In music, *pianissimo* means as soft as possible, like a brush of a feather. *Mezzo piano* means medium soft. *Fortissimo* means to play loudly. Well, our voice is like a musical instrument.

"The first kind of voice is a 0-Inch Voice. It means no talking, no noise. When I want a 0-Inch Voice, I will make a zero with my thumb and all my fingers. You can, too, to remind you.

"The second kind of voice is a 3-Inch Voice. It means that you can talk very, very softly, so your neighbor can hear you, but not the whole class. I will put my three long fingers in front of my mouth to show the 3-Inch Voice.

"The third kind of voice is a 3-Foot Voice. It means that you can talk in a normal voice to people near you. I will put my hands several feet apart as a cue to use a 3-Foot Voice.

(Optional) "Another kind of voice is called 10-Foot or Stage Voice. It's what is used when you are talking to an audience. I will cue this voice by bringing the palm of my hand from my chest out with palm facing up.

"The final kind of voice is a 30-Foot Voice. It is only to be used by adults when there is an emergency. I will cup my hands around my mouth to show a 30-Foot Voice."

The young people asked, "Can we practice our PAX Voices?"

"What a great idea," said the teacher. "We will practice all our PAX Voices, except the 30-Foot Voice."

When the young people did the voices correctly, the teacher praised the class. Over the week, the class practiced quickly going from one voice level to another several times. The children made special posters for the classroom showing the PAX Voices levels.

"What a wonderful school this is," said the young people.

Discuss the story:
Ask the students the following questions. Call on students using PAX Stix, if you like.

1. What change made the school more wonderful?

2. Can you show me a 3-Inch Voice? What is its hand signal?

3. Can you show me a 3-Foot Voice? What is its hand signal?

4. *Optional:* Can you show me a 10-Foot or Stage Voice and its hand signal?

5. Can you show me a 0-Inch Voice? What is its hand signal?

Beat the Timer
Beat the Timer challenges children to complete a task in less time than what is set on the timer. This powerful strategy can increase the accuracy and speed of task completion.

Use these steps in teaching Beat the Timer:

1. Explain the task that you would like the children to do (for example, transition from a math assignment to reading circles or complete a particular writing assignment).

2. Tell the children how long you will give them to complete the task. Set the timer for this amount of time.

3. On "Go," the children strive to do this activity before the timer goes off.

4. If team members complete the task safely and orderly in the allotted amount of time, their team scores a PAX Win.

5. Praise children for beating the timer. Individually recognize children who were especially efficient in getting work done or making a transition.

6. Award prizes to teams who beat the timer.

7. Tip: Wear the timer on a string around your neck or on your belt for easy reach.

Here are examples using Beat the Timer for both fun and work:

- "Let's beat the timer by passing out all our papers in one minute."

- "Now let's see how many can beat the timer by getting their desktops cleaned off in thirty seconds."

- "You have one minute to talk to your neighbor about something you learned today."

- "I'm going to set the timer for us to work the problems in the next five minutes."

- "For a reward, we have two minutes of singing."

- "We have twenty minutes for silent reading. I'll set the timer now."

- "I'm setting a timer for five minutes of rapid writing. You have ten seconds to get ready. When I say 'Go,' start writing."

- "When the timer rings in two minutes, everyone needs to be ready for the science experiment and have the spelling papers put away for grading."

PAX Stix

PAX Stix involves putting the children's names on Popsicle™ or craft sticks, randomly selecting a stick, and calling on the child whose name appears on the stick.

PAX Stix is a teacher-proven, simple practice to improve student attention and participation while reducing classroom disruptions. It is based on the scientific practice of random selection. In the PAX Game, random means that the child who gets called on cannot be predicted. If the students can predict when they will get called on to participate, human nature kicks in. They daydream, act up, or lose attention.

When students don't know when they will be called on, they pay better attention and are less disruptive. Brain-scan research suggests that random calling or stimuli increase the attention circuitry related to language learning important in academics. The same principle is used in computer games to sustain attention (think how much kids pay attention to those games versus school instruction).

Here are simple steps for preparing and using PAX Stix:

1. Purchase a bag of craft or Popsicle™ sticks. (Smaller, two-inch sticks work best.)

2. Put each child's name on one stick.

3. *Optional:* Color code class periods if you teach multiple groups. A dot of marker ink works well. Do not let the children decorate the sticks because then they can tell whose stick you are drawing.

4. Put the sticks in a cup or container that you can easily and quickly reach. Or keep the sticks in your pocket.

5. Once you call on a student, put the stick back in the cup or pocket to keep the students on their toes and paying attention.

6. Use the sticks several times an hour and as needed.

7. A child who cannot answer may ask for a "lifeline" from another student. The other student can answer the question, but the original child must repeat the lifeline answer.

Playing the PAX Game during the Third Week

During the third week, your aim is to make the game run very smoothly. Nothing new needs to be added. Both you and the students are working on making everything "automatic." You may slightly increase the time that the children play the game, if they have been consistently winning at the lesser amount of time. The PAX Game and PAX Cues need to become like habit during this week.

You can probably switch to daily prizes instead of a prize after every game, with an occasional random prize immediately after a game. This is the beginning of learning delayed gratification and "brain building" for long-term self-control.

Starting Peer-to-Peer Tootles during the Fourth Week

During the fourth week, keep up the PAX Game three times a day. If you have not done so, now is the time to experiment with having the prize at the end of the day as a solid practice. You ought to be able to double or triple the time you play the game successfully during easy times now. Continue secret games (with immediate prizes) several times a week.

Peer-to-Peer Tootle Notes

If tattling wears you out, then this is the week to start tootling. Remember, tootles are the opposite of tattles. Tootles are for noticing PAX Leader behaviors of team members and other classmates that make a more wonderful school or classroom.

Peer-to-peer tootles are typically written (or dictated in the case of some children). They can be posted on a Tootle Board for all to see. If you use Tootle Notes consistently, you will be amazed in a few weeks at the positive behavior and goodwill this activity brings out.

Use these steps in teaching Peer-to-Peer Tootle Notes:

1. Make photocopies of the Tootle Note form found in appendix B on page 108. Cut out each note.

2. Read the PAX Tootle Note story found on pages 54–55 in this guide.

3. Explain the meaning of a Tootle Note to your students. Tootles are the opposite of tattles. Tootling is looking for the positive actions of others and telling them about their actions.

4. Give examples of things the children could tootle about (someone does a nice thing for someone else; a person shares something with someone, etc.).

5. Give each student a Tootle Note form. Have them write a Tootle Note to someone in your class. You may want to assign students so that everyone receives a note.

Here are example messages:
- "Thanks for sitting quietly while the teacher was talking."
- "You really helped our team win today by using the correct PAX Voice."
- "You're a PAX Leader, because you helped _____ learn math."

6. Create a display of Tootle Notes in your classroom.

    Optional: Get a can of repositionable spray-mount adhesive, which is rather like the glue on sticky notes. Spray a big sheet of butcher paper, about three feet by four feet or more, labeled Tootle Board. Tape the paper on one of your classroom walls. Now children will be able to "slap" up their notes. No tape, tacks, or pins are needed. The spray glue lasts weeks, although it may need a touch-up if humidity gets extreme.

7. If students post offensive notes, simply remove them without public comment—to avoid accidental reinforcement of negative behavior. If possible, give the offensive note back to the sender to redo in a positive way.

8. Send Home Link Flyer 3 about Tootle Notes (found in appendix B on page 115) to the children's families.

Note: All praise is not created equal. To create behavior change, praise must be directed to *specific* behaviors you want. Praise for something vague works against your goals, as do compliments for possessions or appearance, unless there is a specific rationale for giving them. A tootle is for a specific action or an accomplishment, not a vague compliment.

Tips for Tootling Success

Teach the children to write specific information about what the person did to make more PAX. Tootle Notes say:

- When and where the action happened
- What the person *did* (or didn't do) to earn the Tootle Note
- How the positive action contributes to the common good or PAX

PAX Tootles (A True Story)[14]

Once upon a time, there were thirteen schools. The schools were not good places to be. Grown-ups at the schools were sad and mad. Kids at the schools were sad and mad. Families around the schools were sad and mad. Nobody was glad. Everybody thought those thirteen schools were very, very bad.

People tattled on each other all the time. Kids tattled on other kids. Adults tattled on other adults. People said mean words to each other.

"How can our schools be less bad and more glad?" asked everyone. "We need somebody we can trust to show us a way out of this mess."

Not faraway from the schools was a university. Two professors taught there. One was a man, the other a woman. They liked to help schools, teachers, kids, and families. They were scientists. They studied ways to make schools better places to learn and have fun.

The schools asked the two professors to help them. The professors watched how people at the schools treated each other. Nobody was very nice.

The professors said, "We suggest that the schools conduct an experiment. Let's test to see what happens if we get people thanking each other for being helpful or friendly. When people praise what is good, more good happens. We have a special word for this. It's called tootling. It is the opposite of tattling."

The experiment started. Every day, at each school, students and grown-ups wrote Tootle Notes to each other, to neighbors, and to families. The Tootle Notes began with "Dear _____." The notes thanked people or groups for specific actions and said how the actions were good. The writer either signed it or put

"A Secret Friend" on the bottom of the note. Little kids drew their notes, and sometimes they had help from older kids. Grown-ups wrote down the kind words from the very young children.

The Tootle Notes were posted on boards throughout each school. Some notes were put up in the front office. Some went up in the lunchroom. Others were put up in classrooms or posted in hallways. The schools worked hard at putting up the Tootle Notes. The students helped display them every day.

The teachers realized that the Tootle Notes made writing fun for kids, which was a bonus. The kids liked writing tootles. It helped them make a better world, and they made more friends.

After a month or so, everyone could see that the Tootle Notes made a difference. People started to smile and do more positive things. People were nicer. More work got done. The buildings looked nicer. Families said nicer things to teachers and children. Students did better at school. People stopped tattling so much.

Everyone who visited the schools said, "What a wonderful school."

Discuss the story:
Ask the students the following questions. Call on students using PAX Stix, if you like.

1. What change made the schools more wonderful?

2. What is a tootle?

3. What is the difference between a tootle and a tattle?

4. What is something you could tootle about in our classroom? What positive actions might children or adults do?

Also consider using these other types of Tootle Notes:

- *Home Tootle Notes* are a proven strategy to improve behavior at home and school.[15] Teachers send home a Tootle Note about something good a child has done at school, cueing the adults at home to praise the child for positive behaviors. Try to send five to ten Home Tootle Notes per week (per class not per student). You can use the Tootle Note form provided in this guide or Home Note postcards (purchased separately from Hazelden Publishing).

  It is very important to recognize the *inhibition* of aggressive or disruptive impulses as a positive behavior that is occurring. If a child habitually interrupts every five minutes, and thirty minutes have gone by without interruptions, give the child a Home Tootle Note along with verbal praise for inhibiting the interrupting behavior, and ask the child how he or she did that. (The child may not know, but next time he or she will pay attention.)

- *Family Tootle Notes* are a version that family members write to one another. Families can also use Tootle Notes to inform the school about something children have done well at home. Give bonus **PAX** Wins for any you receive. Promote Family Tootle Notes by sending home the Parent Booklet (described on pages 57–58 in this guide) or pads of notes designed by the children. Have families write Tootle Notes at conferences or open houses.

Beginning "My Wonderful PAX School" Parent Booklet during the Fifth or Sixth Week

During the fifth or sixth week, rotate team membership. Again, try to have equal numbers of shy, aggressive, special education, and regular students on each team. Have the students pick new team names (which must be okayed by the teacher).

If your children seem ready, challenge them to play the game to win a bigger weekly prize rather than daily prizes. Do this with all but your secret games. Continue to award prizes at the end of the day for secret games.

Introduce the "My Wonderful PAX School" Parent Booklet.
The "My Wonderful PAX School" Parent Booklet, along with the Home Link Flyers, is one of your most important tools in encouraging family involvement in the PAX Game. However, just sending home the booklets, without any thought or promotion, will not achieve the total purpose and benefit of the booklet. You will need to carefully introduce the booklet to your students.

Make one copy per student of the "My Wonderful PAX School" Parent Booklet (included in the PAX Game Kit). Staple each copy in three places along the spine to create a booklet.

Send home Home Link Flyer 4 (found in appendix B on page 116) that introduces families to the "My Wonderful PAX School" Parent Booklet. At the same time distribute copies of the Parent Booklet to your students. Explain that the booklet has six chapters with a homework assignment at the end of each chapter.

The students should read and discuss each chapter and do the homework assignment with their parent(s) or guardian(s).

Each chapter is meant to be done on a separate day.

After each chapter, the students should complete and cut out the homework assignment and bring it back to class. You will want to assign due dates for the assignments. Really play up the fact that the children will win special recognition for their teams by completing and returning the homework.

You might choose to have only certain chapters figure into your team contests. The data to be posted are NOT for individual children, but for teams.

Added Suggestions

Enlarge the homework completion form on page 59 in this guide and make one for each PAX team. Post the forms in the classroom so students can keep track of how their team is doing in completing homework.

Give every NEW student a booklet and ask new families to complete it.

If a child comes from a difficult home environment, where it is unlikely that parents or guardians will work through the Parent Booklet, have another community or school adult read the booklet with the child.

Research Note

Specially constructed workbooks in story form have been shown to change children's behavior and family behavior.[16] The PAX Game Parent Booklet is designed to increase imitation of PAX Leader skills, as well as to create an alliance between families and the school. Specially constructed stories, workbooks, and modeling activities can reduce aggressive behavior, increase social competence, and build character,[17] especially when combined with other evidence-based strategies, such as those in the PAX Game.[18]

Follow up on "My Wonderful PAX School" Parent Booklet homework.
Use the form on the next page to chart completion of homework assignments.

Added Suggestion

Also put the information about homework assignments on your classroom Web site or in your classroom newsletter—if you have them.

"My Wonderful PAX School" Parent Booklet Homework

Classroom: _____

PAX Team: _____

CHAPTER	NUMBER RETURNED	PERCENTAGE RETURNED
Chapter 1, "The Idea"		
Chapter 2, "We Think Up the Game"		
Chapter 3, "Our Game Starts Up"		
Chapter 4, "Tootling for PAX"		
Chapter 5, "Playing the PAX Game at Mealtime"		
Chapter 6, "Making Your School and Your World Better"		

Check on the implementation of the Parent Booklet and Home Link Flyers.

The checklist on page 61 will help you make sure the implementation of the "My Wonderful PAX School" Parent Booklet and Home Link Flyers is effective. The Parent Booklet should be studied and used by families over the course of approximately two weeks. Some schools may be able to finish the booklet in one week, but this could be a stretch. Some might take three weeks. Four weeks is a bit too long for continuity and impact.

Research Note

PAX Home Link Flyers are designed to engage families in the adoption, adaptation, and use of PAX Cues and tootles at home. Various studies have shown that specially constructed family-advice flyers can be helpful.[19]

Checklist for Parent Booklet and Home Link Flyer 4 Implementation

TASK TO BE COMPLETED	DATE COMPLETED
1. Send Home Link Flyer 4 to families.	
2. Send Parent Booklet home with due date for chapter 1 assignment.	
3. Post and communicate results of chapter 1 assignment.	
4. Assign due date for chapter 2 homework assignment.	
5. Post and communicate results of chapter 2 assignment.	
6. Assign due date for chapter 3 assignment.	
7. Post and communicate results of chapter 3 assignment.	
8. Assign due date for chapter 4 assignment.	
9. Post and communicate results for chapter 4 assignment.	
10. Assign due date for chapter 5 assignment.	
11. Post and communicate results for chapter 5 assignment.	
12. Assign due date for chapter 6 assignment.	
13. Post and communicate results for chapter 6 assignment.	
14. Celebrate results of Parent Booklet assignments.	

©2003 by Hazelden Foundation. All rights reserved. Duplicating this page for personal or group use is permissible.

Increasing Game Time during the Seventh and Eighth Weeks

Your long-term goal in playing the PAX Game is to reach a point where primary-grade children are able to play the game successfully for fifteen to twenty minutes and intermediate-grade children are able to play successfully for twenty to forty minutes. Some classrooms may be able to play longer, but playing time depends greatly on the mix of children in the classroom.

You may want to add new prizes or an extra dose of Tootle Notes at this time to motivate greater success among your students.

Increasing the Generalization of PAX Skills during the Ninth through Fourteenth Weeks

In the beginning, your students played the PAX Game during "easier-to-use" times, such as independent or paired seatwork. You also played the game during group instruction. Now that your students have increased the amount of time they are able to play the PAX Game with success, they are ready to improve their general ability to inhibit Spleems in more contexts or in more difficult circumstances. Here's how:

- Play the PAX Game during cooperative learning activities or activities that involve movement in the classroom. The children will find this harder. You may need to play shorter games as the children adapt to these new "brain" demands.

- Play the PAX Game during transitions to out-of-classroom activities such as going to the bathroom or going to and from recess, lunch, the library, or the computer lab. Be sure that "violations" of PAX Quiet, PAX Hands, PAX Voices, and, optionally, Beat the Timer are considered in your Spleems count.

Making Habits for the Future in the Fifteenth Week and Beyond

By this time, primary-grade children ought to be able to play the game well for thirty minutes at a time. Intermediate-grade students ought to be up to forty-five to sixty minutes per game.

Also at this point, secret game wins need not have an immediate reward, unless you have a number of special-needs children in your class.

Strive to make the PAX Game a habit with your class. For ideas on how to maintain the game, see chapter 4 in this guide.

If your school is implementing the PAX Game schoolwide, make sure you coordinate your efforts with the efforts of other staff members. This includes training substitute teachers and creating teamwork with special-subjects teachers such as the computer lab specialist, librarian, or music teacher.

Chapter Three

Addressing the Special Needs of Children

This version of the PAX Game is designed for children in grades K–6. With some adaptation, however, you can use the PAX Game with younger children. Also, the PAX Game can be adapted to better meet the needs of special education students as well as students from poverty areas. This chapter contains ideas to address each of these specific audiences.

Adapting the Game for Early Childhood Settings

The PAX Game requires some adaptation to work in an early-childhood setting. Young children have difficulty sitting still, they move around a lot, and their learning activities are much more active. Additionally, these children have less understanding and ability to control their own behavior, particularly if they have not had much adult-supervised training at home. You can adapt the PAX Game to younger children's needs by:

- Using more stories or concrete objects to model appropriate behavior. Combine this with songs or choral responses to aid children's understanding.

- Rehearsing the PAX Game and the type of behavior you want over and over. Give the children feedback as they practice. Practice the game in more and more natural circumstances until the children are able to control their own behavior even during free times.

- Letting them know when you are using a PAX Game Cue, such as PAX Hands or PAX Voices.

- Creating two puppets. Call one PAX and the other Spleem. PAX needs to be cute. Spleem needs to be ugly. The puppets can be made from paper bags, socks, or gloves using fabric scraps and a glue gun or a needle and thread.

- Using the puppets to demonstrate the concept of PAX (behaviors that make the classroom safe, happy, and productive) and Spleems (behaviors that make people feel unhappy, unproductive, unhealthy, afraid, or disliked).

- Using the puppets to model PAX behavior. For example, have the PAX puppet say something kind to the Spleem puppet and ask the children if the behavior was PAX or a Spleem. Praise the children for a correct response.

Once younger children understand what PAX and Spleems are, you will want to train them in the basics of the game. Do this in slower and smaller steps than you would with elementary-age children. Here are basic guidelines:

- Young children are highly mobile. Make sure the children wear team wristbands that can easily be seen by staff in the room. Elastic hair bands or PAX Leader name tags work well, too. Do not use name tags with sharp pins.

- Make sure you have an easy way of marking Spleems while you are moving around the room. You might make bead counters for the teams using pipe cleaners and beads around your wrist. Another solution is to put masking-tape strips on your sleeve. Make marks on the tape strips. Then put the totals on the Spleems Tally Sheet. You could also carry a small Spleems Tally Sheet with you on a clipboard.

- First practice stopping Spleems for a minute or so using the timer. Do this during times when you know the children will be most able to control their behavior, such as when sitting in a circle on the floor or at tables. DO NOT start with hard situations.

- For winning teams use very simple activity prizes lasting a few moments, such as jumping up and down, whistling, or humming a song.

- Strictly enforce Spleems in these brief simple situations. Do so with a light touch, voice, and heart, however. DO NOT yell, condemn, or make a scene about a Spleem. The idea is to make sure the children have a clear understanding of how to control the simplest of Spleems, such as blurting out or jiggling somebody.

- Move up to more complex situations and tasks as the children show they can master the situation and skill. Do not rush too fast if the children are having a problem.

- Constantly ALERT children to Spleems early on when not playing the game. For example, "I see some Spleems with people not sharing the blocks. PAX Leaders share their blocks. Oh, good, I see boys and girls starting PAX now."

- Link stories you are reading to the PAX Game. Highlight when a story character is being a PAX Leader and when he or she is making a Spleem. Have children "vote" with their thumbs up or down whether the stories show a Spleem or PAX.

Note: Some of the above procedures are also effective with older students who are more immature or who have symptoms of attention deficit–hyperactivity disorder.

Adaptations for Children with Special Needs, 504 Plans, and Mental Health Issues

Children with special needs (for example, attention deficit disorder, oppositional disorders, autism, or mood disorders such as depression, anxiety, or bipolar disorder) are not just "being bad" when everything you try seems unsuccessful in helping them to show more positive behavior. Many people don't know that if you take a picture of these children's brains using a special camera, you will find large areas that function poorly or not at all.

The PAX Game mimics the behavioral effects of the drug Ritalin™ commonly used with many of these youngsters. By using the PAX Game, these special-needs children can be trained either to function better or to compensate, so their chances of living a normal life are much improved.

Here are specific tips for using the PAX Game with this group of children:

- When teams are formed, be sure to distribute special-needs children evenly among the teams. If one team has a disproportionate number of impulsive children, it is wise to redistribute the teams earlier than you had planned.

- If possible, preteach the PAX Game to special-needs students, and have them be part of teaching the game to the rest of the class.

- If you have several special-needs children or their problems with impulse control are particularly severe, it is important to start by playing the game for very short time periods. Do this so they and their teammates experience success right away. The joy they will get from being on a winning team will far exceed the joy of whatever the reward is—but the reward must be given immediately, anyway.

- Encourage peers to coach and praise these children. For example, peers can praise special-needs children for helping the team to win.

- Assign students who are more mature to be special PAX Coaches.

They can give nonverbal cues to special-needs students to help keep them from making Spleems.

- Although it may eventually be necessary, don't be too quick to assign a special-needs child to be on a team by himself or herself. It would be better to shorten the time of play so that the child can experience success. Use the solo-team intervention instead for the more antisocial students who deliberately subvert the game to express their bravado.

Children who have special designations or needs may benefit by added support. For example, children who are especially disruptive may need to practice playing the game in a smaller setting, such as playtime with a counselor. They might need more feedback during those sessions. Skills learned in the smaller setting might be transferred to the classroom by having the counselor coach the child during regular classroom instruction using the small Stop Spleems and Go PAX signs.

Children who are depressed or very shy or who have been victimized or witnessed serious trauma may benefit from being chosen for one of the more visible team jobs, such as PAX Captain. Being in such roles reduces their victimization by other children, improves their social status, and lifts their negative mood.

Children who are extremely impulsive benefit by having their positive behavior recognized more frequently. Send Tootle Notes about these children as often as you can. Children with impaired social competence will benefit by special practice in writing and giving Tootle Notes to peers and adults. In rare cases, some children with unusual diagnoses prefer being on their own team, and may do better.

All of these activities fall into the purview of services justified under special education programs, 504 Plans, or mental health interventions. Also, the PAX Game, especially PAX Cues and tootles, is a practical strategy to write specifically into an Individual Education Plan (IEP) or 504 Plan.

Children Who Intentionally Sabotage the Game

Occasionally, a child may delight in repeatedly sabotaging the game, which is quite different from a child who gives up after "losing" a particular game. Typically, a child who does a simple "I hate this game" is frustrated and will turn around the next game. Some temperamental behavior is to be expected, especially among children who are used to getting their own way with adults and peers. Their temperamental outbursts are an attempt to get control back. Hold your course steady in these cases.

The child who delights in making sure his or her team fails is a different case. Typically, such children have a long history of accidental reinforcement by peers for deviant behavior. So, invoke PAX Game Rule 101 and Rule 102 as previously discussed on pages 30–31.

Children in High-Crime or Poverty Areas

Sometimes it is helpful to use material things (stickers, candies, pencils) as rewards, particularly when just starting the game. This is especially the case for children who are most "at risk," but all children will appreciate the occasional "goodie." Gradually, as the year progresses, add more activity rewards to the mix.

If your school is in a low-income neighborhood, consider having pretzels or popcorn on hand *not* as a reward, but as an expression of daily nurturance and care. Many times, wiggly behavior is related to empty tummies. Many middle-class or upper-class adults who work in areas with a high rate of poverty may not understand that presentation of food items is very appropriate.

Remember the caution of Ruby Payne (educator, author, and trainer), who is famous for her insights into issues of wealth: Upper-class folks ask, "Is the food pretty?" Middle-class folks ask, "Is it tasty?" Poor people ask, "Is there enough?" Children in poverty, who are not being properly fed, have a higher need for instant gratification. They also are likely to perceive the world as dangerous and unpredictable. Such perceived stress literally can "turn on" the genes that crave dopamine or reward in humans.

Children in poverty areas often witness horrible human predatory behavior. For example, 20 percent of seven-year-olds in some U. S. inner cities have witnessed a homicide. Mother Nature alters brain circuits in such circumstances, as a defense mechanism for survival. Distrusting other people, especially adults, is wired into about 50 percent of these children. The shift in brain chemistry and even structure is shocking. Hyperactivity, desire for immediate reward, disrespect, and aggression are common. The PAX Game and related tools will help address these issues.

Children who live in poor neighborhoods are also exposed to very high levels of lead. The lead is not so much in the building paint as it is carried in the air from soil contaminated by past manufacturing or haphazard waste disposal. Such children may have as much as ten picograms per deciliter of lead in their blood, a level that seriously interferes with dopamine transmission and neuron development even though it is not technically considered seriously toxic (that is, causing death or deformity).

The net result is impulsive, hyperactive, and aggressive behavior—not to mention decreased academic performance. Many ill-informed people add insult to injury by yelling, screaming, or threatening such children in a desperate attempt to control behavior. This creates post-traumatic reactions among children who are biologically vulnerable and actually makes the impulsivity and need for immediate reinforcement worse. The PAX Game has worked well in areas with high-lead levels.

Scientifically valid behavioral practices such as the PAX Game are medically and ethically indicated for children exposed to toxic substances and toxic human interactions that assault their brains and behavior. Of course, other interventions are needed as well.

Chapter Four

Continuing Your PAX Good Behavior Game Efforts

Without proper planning, even the best efforts at playing the PAX Game may fade over time. To help you avoid this problem, this chapter contains recommendations to keep your PAX Game efforts going.

Creating Success between Games

How do you increase positive behavior between PAX Games? Use one of these two strategies: PAX Tax or PAX Timer Surprise. Which one will work better depends somewhat on your students.

PAX Tax

The PAX Tax can be used concurrently with the PAX Game as a way to gain better control of unruly classrooms. Use the same teams as you would for a PAX Game. All team members start the day with a set of three slips of paper, which are laminated. Use a different color paper for each team. If you have teams of different sizes, make sure you give out an equal number of slips to each team. Place one slip (the tax) from each team in a winner's bucket or bowl. During the day, when you are NOT playing the PAX Game, take a slip from a child whenever he or she commits a Spleem and put it aside, not in the winner's bucket. Non-emotional removal of the slips of paper is vital.

At the end of the day, put all the slips left on the students' desks in the winner's bowl, along with the starter slips. The starter slips guarantee that each team has a chance to win even if all its individual slips were lost by Spleeming. The team with the most slips left has the best chance to win, of course.

Close your eyes and draw a slip from the bowl. Award a prize that is "worth winning" to the selected team or add the PAX Tax win to the team's total PAX Wins for the week.

If your class is quite difficult, the prize should be awarded at the end of the day. If a team wins both best PAX Game score and PAX Tax on the same day, you may wish to double the prize.

PAX Timer Surprise

Set a timer to go off at random times throughout the day, but NOT while you are playing the PAX Game. Before playing PAX Timer Surprise, draw a PAX Stix. Do not tell the children whose name is on the stick. When the timer goes off, if that child is showing PAX, his or her team gets a Spleem *subtracted* from the PAX Wins Scoreboard. PAX Timer Surprise is simpler to do than PAX Tax and will work for most classrooms.

Nonclassroom Transitions

Once you have effectively implemented the PAX Game in your classroom, you can begin to play the game while the students are transitioning to the bathroom, going to recess, or going to the lunchroom.

If something is observed in a bathroom (which is where about 40 percent of all acts of aggression happen), give each misbehaving student's team a Splat—which is a double Spleem. This may be applied to a game in progress or to the next PAX Game you play in your classroom.

Schoolwide Implementation

Once you have mastered the use of the PAX Game in your classroom, you may want to encourage other teachers or your entire school staff to use the PAX Game. For more information about implementing a schoolwide PAX Game effort, order the *PAX Good Behavior Game* Schoolwide Implementation Guide available from Hazelden Publishing at 1-800-328-9000.

Keeping the Effort Strong throughout the Year

It is difficult to keep any new strategy, even a positive one like the PAX Game, going without special effort. There are key times during the school year when you will need to reinforce the principles of this game.

Testing Time

Some teachers say, "Oh, we can't do any of that PAX Game stuff during test time." The reverse is true. Test time is just the time to play the game. Children who are struggling academically tend to misbehave under the stress of testing. They also get more impulsive. The PAX Game is a proven cure for impulsivity and will create a less stressful classroom environment.

Use Beat the Timer to help the children practice for timed tests. Sending home special Tootle Notes during test time—praising diligence and attentiveness—will help motivate children to do their best. Use the PAX Cues and stop-and-go signs to help students maintain attention while listening to test instructions or taking tests.

Before the End of School

Some teachers and schools let things slide the last month, weeks, or days of school. This cheats the children of learning. Instead, create exciting PAX Game competitions between teams during this time of year. If your school is implementing the game schoolwide, create competitions between classes and grades.

The contest prizes may include a whole week of being first for lunch, having ice-cream sodas, or having a comedy team or magician come to your room. One school used being able to chew gum the last day of school as a reward. The prospect of earning this prize motivated the students to work diligently. Another class was able to wear pajamas the last day of school for having the most PAX Wins for two weeks. These kids worked hard up to the last moment, and they also had the top test scores in the district.

The "Boring" Phenomenon

Children who express low tolerance for boredom are at a very high risk of being disruptive in school—just to get a thrill. Such children are also more likely to experiment with or use tobacco, alcohol, or other drugs, or bring a weapon to school.

Some children are wired to need more stimulation and reward. Their brains are that way from birth. Here are some ways to keep these children involved in the PAX Game:

- *Create PAX Game treasure chests.* In cooperation with other teachers who are using the PAX Game, place different prize or reward ideas in a box or treasure chest. Every week or month, rotate the treasure chests among classrooms. This provides new and exciting incentives to play the game. Be aware that prizes that work with primary grades may not work with intermediate grades.

- *Offer mystery bonus prizes.* Think up some extra-special prizes, like having a banana-split party, being on TV, or having a local sports star come to the classroom. Place descriptions of these special prizes in envelopes. Have representatives from each team (or class, if you are playing the game schoolwide) randomly draw a mystery prize envelope. The mystery prize is not revealed until the day the wins are tallied and winning teams receive a prize. All of this takes some logistical planning, but mystery bonus prizes are very powerful in producing positive behavior.

Involving New Students

In a year's time, many schools have a 25 percent or more turnover in their student population. Studies have shown that children who move from school to school often have more behavioral difficulties. Thus, all of the efforts your class works hard to achieve can be diluted by the influx of new students.

It's important to have a strong new-student orientation program that includes learning the PAX Game. Here are some orientation ideas:

- Give new students and their parents a copy of the Parent Booklet, and show them the PAX Game Video, if you purchased it.

- Appoint another student to be a PAX Leader Buddy to help the new child learn the game, and to give the child tootles throughout his or her first days at school. If the child has special needs, also offer individual PAX Game coaching right away.

Involving Other Staff Members

Most classroom teachers have other adults who work with their students. Be sure to involve them in your PAX Game efforts. Here are some ideas:

- If you have aides or classroom volunteers, train them to use the PAX Game and to write Tootle Notes. This will maintain consistency in your classroom. You might also prepare a "bag of tricks" (a bag of special prizes) for these helpers to use with the children.

- Encourage special-subjects teachers to get their own PAX Game Kit. Encourage your music, art, physical education, or computer lab teacher to use the PAX Game with your children when they are in your room or have your students. That way, children are consistently using the game in all their classes.

- Prepare a guest teacher package. Make the PAX Game part of your substitute teacher plans. Appoint some children to explain the PAX Game to your substitutes and to assist in playing the game. Give bonus points to winning teams while you are away. Designate the instruction of the game, cues, and tootles to each of the team PAX Captains.

CHAPTER FIVE

Evaluating the Impact of the PAX Good Behavior Game

Before you started playing the PAX Game, you spent time getting baseline data on your class, including the number of Spleems committed during three, fifteen-minute periods. After playing the PAX Game for about four weeks, you will want to evaluate the impact of the game on your class's behavior. This chapter contains tools to help you do this. Once you begin to measure positive results, send Home Link Flyer 5 (found in appendix B on page 117) to families to tell them about the children's progress.

PAX Wins Graph

The most important measure of success is the total number of PAX Wins or total number of PAX Minutes being accumulated by your students. For each team, create simple line graphs for your class totals of PAX Wins and PAX Minutes and chart results every week. Over time, you should see an increase in both totals for your class. Share these measurements of success with your building administrators.

PAX Yesterday Survey

The PAX Yesterday Survey is a simple survey that can be filled out by students in third grade or above. Have the students fill out the survey before you begin playing the game, and then periodically after you have started playing the game. A copy of the survey is provided in appendix E on page 137 of this guide. It will give you a student perspective on changes in behavior due to playing the PAX Game.

The following tools will provide you with more in-depth evaluation, if desired. Use them to establish your baseline data and to measure progress periodically.

Strengths and Difficulties Questionnaire

The Strengths and Difficulties Questionnaire (SDQ) is a brief behavioral screening questionnaire. It can be completed in five minutes by the parents or teachers of children ages four to sixteen. There is also a self-report version for children ages eleven to sixteen.[20] Download the questionnaire, including scoring procedures, at www.sdqinfo.com (a printable scoring version) or www.youthinmind.net (an online scoring version).

Precision Spleems Count and Planned Activity Check

The Precision Spleems Count measures how many disruptions there are in a class. The Planned Activity Check measures to what degree students are engaged in learning.

Measuring Disruptions

The simplest of measures is how many disruptions are happening in the class.

1. Using the Spleems Observation Form found in appendix E on page 139, the observer or observers fill in the total number of students in the classroom at the start of the observation and the number present at the end of fifteen minutes.

   Note: The classroom teacher will naturally be anxious for his or her students to do well—and thus might be inclined to overlook Spleems. For this reason, the observer should not be the teacher. Instead, the observer(s) might be an administrator, another teacher, a classroom aide, or a college student.

2. The observers sit in a spot that enables them to see and hear the whole class, without interfering in class activities. The observers do not talk or interact with the students or the teacher when observing.

3. The observers should use either a stopwatch (which can be on a wristwatch) or a wall clock with a second hand.

4. The observers count the number of Spleems in a one-minute interval and place a hash mark or check on the form for each Spleem. They also indicate the type of activity being done. They continue doing this for fifteen minutes.

5. The observers compute the rate of Spleems per hour per student. For example, in one fifteen-minute interval, observers noted a total of 45 Spleems in Mrs. Heil's class. There were 30 students in the classroom at the outset of the observation and 25 students at the end, for an average of 27.5 students in the classroom during this period.

$$(30 + 25 = 55 \div 2 = 27.5)$$

The rate of disruptions per hour per student would be 6.4.

$$(45 \div 27.5 = 1.6 \times 4 = 6.4)$$

The observers should graph the data as appropriate.

6. Schedule the next observation.

Measuring Engaged Learning

If a class is not very disruptive or inattentive, then measuring actual engagement may be more useful than measuring disruptions.

1. Using the Planned Activity Check form found in appendix E on page 141, the observer or observers total the number of students in the classroom during each minute interval during the fifteen-minute period.

2. The observers sit in a spot that enables them to see and hear the whole class, without interfering. The observers do not talk or interact with the students or the teacher when observing.

3. The observers should use either a stopwatch (which can be on a wristwatch) or a wall clock with a second hand.

4. The observers count the number of children fully engaged in the lesson for one minute and write the number on the form. They also indicate the type of activity being done. Observers should be very strict in their definition of "engaged." If the planned activity requires that the students be looking at the teacher, looking away should not be counted as engaged. If the planned activity requires that the students be focused on a worksheet, doodling or looking at the ceiling should not be counted as engaged.

5. The observers continue until fifteen minutes are finished. They then calculate the percentage of children who were engaged during each minute by dividing the number engaged in learning by the number in the room. For example, during minute one in Mrs. Heil's classroom, there were 30 children, 25 of whom were engaged in learning. The percentage for this minute is 83 ($25 \div 30 = 83\%$).

    The observers next total all the percentages and divide by 15 to get the average percent engaged during observation.

6. The observers graph the data as appropriate.

7. Schedule the next observation.

APPENDIX A

PAX Good Behavior Game Glossary

PAX Good Behavior Game Glossary

This glossary defines the key words used in the *PAX Good Behavior Game*.

Beat the Timer – Children are challenged to make a transition to another activity or to get work done in a certain amount of time, indicated by the use of the timer.

Go PAX Signs – Signs that the teacher uses to tell children they are acting in positive ways. The teacher taps on a Go PAX sign whenever he or she sees a child doing a positive action.

PAX – A Latin word that means people have productivity, peace, happiness, and health.

PAX Captains – A team job where students tell their team members when it's time to play the game, announce total games won, and announce prizes.

PAX Coaches – A team job where students give nonverbal cues to fellow team members when playing the game.

PAX Go Getters – A team job where students pick up handouts or classroom supplies for their team members, whenever directed to do so by the teacher.

PAX Good Behavior Game – A research-based practice that classroom teachers can use to decrease discipline problems and increase learning.

PAX Hands – Children keep their hands at their sides or behind their backs when moving from activity to activity.

PAX Leader – A person who helps increase the productivity, peace, health, and happiness of a classroom, a home, or the world.

PAX Motto – A statement that children recite that reinforces their commitment to behave in positive ways. The PAX Motto is "I better my world, and I better myself."

PAX Promise – A pledge that children are encouraged to recite and live by in order to increase positive behavior in the classroom. *(The PAX Promise can be found on page 101 of this guide.)*

PAX Quiet – The teacher makes a "peace sign" hand signal and blows the harmonica to get children to quiet down and pay attention.

PAX Reminders – A team job where students remind other team members of their roles and jobs.

PAX Stix – Children's names are written on Popsicle™ sticks and placed in a cup. The teacher calls on children based on the PAX Stix chosen from the cup. This activity challenges students to be ready at all times to be called on.

PAX Tootle Notes – Notes that children give to each other, complimenting each other on their positive behavior. Teachers, other school staff, and parents can also write Tootle Notes.

PAX Tootlers – A team job where students recognize the positive actions of their team members and encourage team members to send Tootle Notes to each other.

PAX Voices – Children are asked to speak at appropriate levels of volume. There are different levels of PAX Voices, depending on where the children are and what they are doing.

PAX Wins Scoreboard – Found on page 97 of this guide, this form can be used to record PAX Game Wins by class teams.

Splams – Deliberately making Spleems in order to get attention or throw the game. Team members may be asked to play solo if they splam.

Splats – Splats are given for especially disruptive behavior, such as destroying costly property or fighting and causing injury. Splats count twice as much as a normal Spleem.

Spleems – Things or actions that get in the way of PAX or stop PAX from happening (for example, not listening, interrupting, saying mean things to others).

Stop Spleems Signs – Signs that the teacher uses to tell children they are acting in negative ways. The teacher taps on a Stop Spleems sign whenever he or she sees a child making a Spleem.

Tootling – Tootling is the opposite of tattling. It is telling people about the *positive* actions of others.

APPENDIX B

PAX Good Behavior Game Forms and Tools

Fidelity and Dose Checklist, 91

See, Hear, Feel, Do Poster, 93

Spleems Tally Sheet, 96

PAX Wins Scoreboard, 97

PAX Game Job Cards, 98

PAX Promise, 101

PAX Quiet Sign, 102

PAX Hands Sign, 103

PAX Voices Sign, 104

Large Stop Spleems Sign, 105

Large Go PAX Sign, 106

Small Stop Spleems and Go PAX Signs, 107

PAX Tootle Note, 108

Sample Informational Letter, 109

Home Link Flyers 1–5, 110

Fidelity and Dose Checklist

All of the PAX interventions need fidelity (using the PAX Game as it was designed to be used) and dose (using the PAX Game consistently and daily) to produce results. Proper dose and fidelity are needed in using all the PAX Game procedures to achieve the maximum benefits for the students, teachers, and school community.

Check these lists on a regular basis to make sure you are applying the right amount of fidelity and dose to achieve needed results.

FIDELITY OR ADOPTION	**DOSAGE OR FREQUENCY OF USE**
PAX GOOD BEHAVIOR GAME—BASIC STEPS	
☐ PAX Game posters and forms used ☐ Teams used/rotated ☐ Timer used ☐ PAX Promise used (optional) ☐ Rules to increase PAX and decrease Spleems developed ☐ Prizes used ☐ "My Wonderful PAX School" story read ☐ Stickers used ☐ Home Link Flyers used ☐ Game jobs assigned ☐ Pretraining conducted for any special-needs children who need it ☐ Mystery prizes introduced ☐ PAX Tax or PAX Timer Surprise used ☐ New prizes introduced or prizes changed often ☐ Rule 101 (solo-team rule) and Rule 102 invoked (if needed) ☐ Special-needs children coached or practiced with	☐ Game played three times per day openly, increasing time with success up to thirty to sixty minutes per game depending on age ☐ Secret game played for ten to fifteen minutes, once a day ☐ PAX Wins and PAX Minutes posted/announced after each game ☐ Teams rotated monthly with balanced membership ☐ Brief daily prizes used in first month or two ☐ Weekly prizes awarded ☐ Stickers used ten times in class ☐ PAX Game jobs rotated weekly ☐ Spleems accurately scored 85 percent of the time ☐ Spleems responded to unemotionally 95 percent of the time by adults ☐ Game played across different activities every week to promote generalization ☐ Timer or timekeeper used each game ☐ Prizes rotated each week or month

Fidelity and Dose Checklist *continued*

FIDELITY OR ADOPTION	DOSAGE OR FREQUENCY OF USE
PAX CUES (PAX QUIET, PAX HANDS, PAX VOICES)	
☐ PAX Quiet taught and practiced ☐ PAX Hands taught and practiced ☐ PAX Voices taught and practiced ☐ Beat the Timer taught and practiced ☐ Stop-and-go signs taught and practiced ☐ PAX Stix taught and practiced ☐ Parent Booklet sent home ☐ Home Link Flyers sent	☐ PAX Quiet used during 85 percent of quiet transitions, with or without harmonica ☐ PAX Hands used daily in hall transitions ☐ Beat the Timer used daily in classroom activities beyond PAX Game ☐ PAX Voices used daily ☐ Stop-and-go signs used daily
PAX HOME TOOTLES	
☐ Home Tootle Notes used ☐ *Optional:* Home Notes postcards purchased and used	☐ Teacher sends home Tootle Notes with one or more teams one or more times per week
PEER-TO-PEER TOOTLE NOTES	
☐ PAX Tootle Notes available ☐ PAX Tootle Notes taught	☐ PAX Tootle Board messages changed at least once per month ☐ Each child "writes" and receives one Tootle Note per week (based on grade)

See	
Hear	
Feel	
Do	

See

Hear

Feel

Do

Spleems Tally Sheet

Copy and post a chart for each game.

NO SPLEEMS

Spleems are actions that block productivity, peace, health, or happiness.

	TOTAL SPLEEMS
TEAM NAME AND COLOR ☆	
TEAM NAME AND COLOR ☆	
TEAM NAME AND COLOR ☆	
TEAM NAME AND COLOR ☆	

- Record Spleems for one game in the far right column.
- Declare winners.
- Erase recorded Spleems and start a new game.
- If you have more than four teams, cut and tape two charts together.
- Be sure to mark wins on the PAX Wins Scoreboard.

Respond to Spleems very matter-of-factly. Do not respond with high emotion or nagging. Just notice and record.

PAX Wins Scoreboard

Copy and post a chart for each team per week.

Team Name: _____ Week of: _____

MONDAY		TUESDAY		WEDNESDAY		THURSDAY		FRIDAY	
WINS		WINS		WINS		WINS		WINS	
PAX Minutes:	Spleems:	PAX Minutes:	Spleems:	PAX Minutes:	Spleems:	PAX Minutes:	Spleems:	PAX Minutes:	Spleems:

Total Weekly Wins: _____

Total Weekly PAX Minutes: _____

Total Weekly Spleems: _____

For each game a team wins, place a sticker or star on the scoreboard.

For each game a team wins, write the total number of minutes the game was played in the PAX Minutes column.

For every game, write the number of Spleems in the Spleems column.

There will be several numbers each day because multiple games are played.

©2003 by Hazelden Foundation. All rights reserved. Duplicating this page for personal or group use is permissible.

PAX Game Job Cards

Make a copy of each card for every team. Laminate the cards.

PAX TEAM CAPTAIN

As your PAX Team Captain, your job is to:

1. Let your team know when your teacher tells you it is time to play a PAX Game.

2. Make a star on the PAX Wins Scoreboard when your team wins.

3. Tell your team the number of minutes won for the game and the total number of minutes won for the week.

4. Tell your team members what they have won and help pass out the prizes, if needed.

PAX TOOTLER

As the PAX Tootler, your job is to:

1. Be on the lookout for team members doing PAX actions.

2. Tell the teacher when a team member does a positive action.

3. Have team members write Tootle Notes to each other.

4. Tell the teacher when a member from another team does a positive action.

©2003 by Hazelden Foundation. All rights reserved. Duplicating this page for personal or group use is permissible.

PAX Game Job Cards *continued*

Make a copy of each card for every team. Laminate the cards.

PAX COACH

As the PAX Coach, your job is to:

1. Set an example by showing positive actions.

2. Help fellow team members to *not* Spleem by:
   - Making the hand signs for PAX Quiet and PAX Voices to remind team members to show PAX actions.
   - Touching the Go PAX sign on a team member's desk or table if he or she is showing PAX.
   - Touching the Stop Spleems sign on a team member's desk or table if he or she is doing a Spleem.

PAX GO GETTER

As the PAX Go Getter, your job is to:

1. Get pencils, books, paper, and other supplies for your team when your teacher says, "Go and get your _____ ."

2. Hand out supplies to your team members.

3. Help when the teacher asks for someone to help from each team.

4. Pick up worksheets, tests, and other classwork from team members and turn them in when told to do so by the teacher.

5. Pick up supplies from your team and return them to their places when told to do so by the teacher.

PAX Game Job Cards *continued*

Make a copy of each card for every team. Laminate the cards.

PAX REMINDER

As the PAX Reminder, your job is to:

⭐ 1 Know which team member is your PAX Captain, PAX Coach, PAX Tootler, and PAX Go Getter. Watch these students do their jobs. Tell them when they are doing their jobs well.

⭐ 2 Remind the PAX Captain, PAX Coach, PAX Tootler, and PAX Go Getter of what they are supposed to do.

⭐ 3 *Optional:* Help lead the PAX Promise.

PAX Promise . . .

I am a PAX Leader, as you will plainly see.
So I better my world and I better me.

I honor good acts, offer help,
and stop harm and blame.

I make my amends and rejoin the game.

I find trusted guides to show me a PAX way.

I strive to improve, a little each day.

I am proud to be a PAX Leader—at school,
at home, in the world, and at play.

PAX Quiet

STOP whatever you are doing.

Stop talking.

Raise hand with PAX Quiet sign.

Eyes on the adult.

PAX Hands

PAX HANDS NEVER HARM.

PAX Hands at your side.

PAX Hands held together behind your back.

PAX Voices

0-inch voice = no talking

3-inch voice = whispering

3-foot voice = talking

10-foot voice = stage/presentation voice

30-foot voice = only used by adults in emergencies

STOP SPLEEMS

GO
PAX

Small Stop Spleems and Go PAX Signs

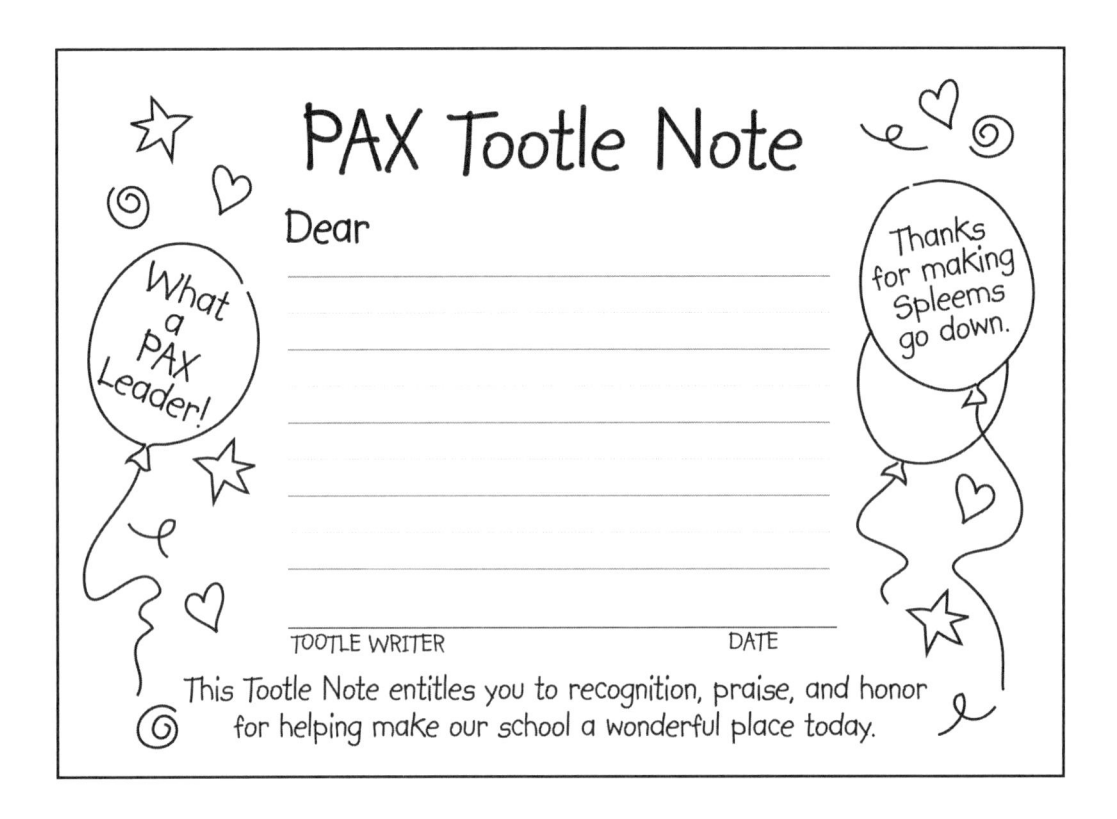

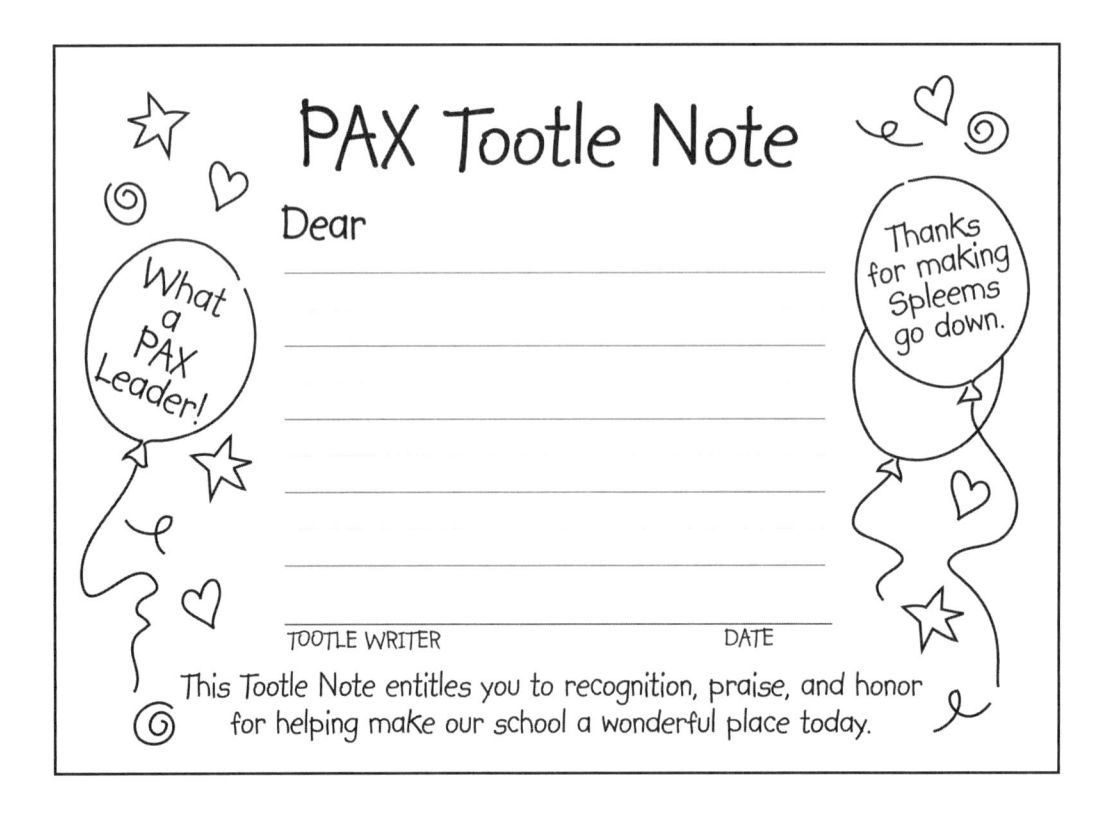

PAX Tootle Note

PAX Tootle Note

Dear _____

What a PAX Leader!

Thanks for making Spleems go down.

TOOTLE WRITER _____ DATE _____

This Tootle Note entitles you to recognition, praise, and honor for helping make our school a wonderful place today.

PAX Tootle Note

Dear _____

What a PAX Leader!

Thanks for making Spleems go down.

TOOTLE WRITER _____ DATE _____

This Tootle Note entitles you to recognition, praise, and honor for helping make our school a wonderful place today.

Sample Informational Letter

Use this letter when you need to share information about the PAX Game with others.

SCHOOL, DISTRICT, OR ORGANIZATIONAL LETTERHEAD

Name
Address
City, State, ZIP Code

RE: Information about the *PAX Good Behavior Game*

Dear _____ ,

Imagine if you found a simple, inexpensive tool that could positively change the lives of all the students in a classroom, at a school, or in a community! Such a tool is the *PAX Good Behavior Game.* Many scientists have proven that this game can:

- Dramatically improve time for teaching and learning.
- Reduce classroom disruptions and disrespect—including bullying and other acts of aggression.
- Reduce students' lifetime problems with tobacco, alcohol, and other drug use.
- Improve the well-being of special-needs children, including those with attention deficit–hyperactivity disorder and conduct disorders.
- Reduce the need for behavior interventions that drain educational resources and taxpayers' dollars.
- Help meet the needs of state and federal education mandates.

The *PAX Good Behavior Game* teaches children to be fully engaged in learning, while reducing disruptions or inattention. Children learn this skill in a fun, interactive way during regular instruction. No extra time is needed to play this game.

I would love to share more information about the *PAX Good Behavior Game* with you, and how I am using it in my classroom. If interested, contact me at _____ .

Sincerely,

(Your name)

Home Link Flyer 1

Introduction to the PAX Good Behavior Game

Dear Family,

Imagine if you found a simple, inexpensive tool that could positively change the lives of all the students in a classroom, at a school, or in a community! We are using such a tool, called the *PAX Good Behavior Game,* in our classroom.

Benefits of the *PAX Good Behavior Game*

The *PAX Good Behavior Game* is the culmination of more than thirty years of scientific study by many investigators. Approximately twenty published studies show that playing the PAX Game leads to reduced classroom disruptions, fewer symptoms of inattention and impulsivity, reduced aggression, fewer referrals and suspensions, more time for teaching and learning, and reduced need for special education or mental health services. There is also evidence that students who play the PAX Game are less likely to use alcohol, tobacco, and other drugs later in life.

What Is the *PAX Good Behavior Game*?

The PAX Game, as children typically call it, is a simple classroom strategy, used during regular instruction. No extra time is needed. Children help define the rules of the classroom to create a more "wonderful school."

Children are placed on teams, which are chosen by the teacher. About three times per day, the teacher sets a timer. While the timer is ticking, the teacher will conduct the class just like normal. If a child does something that gets in the way of the vision of the "wonderful school," then the child's team gets a foul—which the children call a "Spleem."

When the timer rings, the teacher counts up the number of Spleems. If a team has three or fewer Spleems, it wins the game. All teams can win. Simple prizes are awarded to each winning team. After a while, prizes are only awarded at the end of the day.

The PAX Game helps children exercise the portion of the brain that controls impulsivity. During the game, the children learn to support one another rather than make fun of each other. All of this helps to reduce inattention and disruptions, which, in turn, enhances learning.

Talk to your child about the game. He or she can tell you all about Spleems and PAX Wins!

Who Endorses the Game?

The *Good Behavior Game* is endorsed or recommended by the Office of the U. S. Surgeon General, the Center on Substance Abuse Prevention, and other federal, state, and nonprofit organizations.

Can Families Use the PAX Game at Home?

Each family will receive additional Home Link Flyers that give more information on how to play the game. You will also receive a special booklet called "My Wonderful PAX School." Spend time reading and discussing this booklet with your child.

What Can a Family Do to Support the Effort?

First, ask your child about the PAX Game in his or her classroom. Second, praise your child and his or her friends for doing well at the game. Third, use the Home Link Flyer ideas at home. Fourth, let us know what changes you see in your child or the other children at our school.

How Soon Will the PAX Game Benefit My Child's Classroom?

If the game is consistently used, you can expect to see benefits in a month or so.

Thank you for taking the time to keep informed about our efforts to make our classroom and school even better.

Sincerely,

Home Link Flyer 2

PAX Cues Information

Dear Family,

During the next few weeks of playing the PAX Game, we will be learning to use cues for various behaviors and activities in class. These are called PAX Cues. They are designed to reduce disruptions, increase time for instruction, and help foster an even more wonderful classroom and school. Over the next week or two ask your child about these cues, and praise your child for using them.

CUE	WHAT IS IT?	WHAT ARE THE BENEFITS?
PAX Quiet	• PAX Quiet is used to quiet the class, get children's attention, or get them ready for learning. • The PAX Quiet signal is a two-fingered peace sign along with a short note on a harmonica or other pleasant sound. **Children earn recognition for quick responses to the cue.**	• Reduces the transition time from one task to the next from minutes to seconds. • May provide as much as an hour or more time for learning daily. • Makes adults and children calmer.
PAX Hands	• PAX Hands are used when walking in the halls, standing in line, or other places where pushing or shoving might happen. • PAX Hands are held at one's side or clasped in the small of the back. **Adults will praise and recognize PAX Hands at school.**	• Reduces pushing and shoving. • Reduces running in the halls. • Reduces injuries. • Reduces fighting, taunting, teasing, and bullying.

Home Link Flyer 2—page 2

CUE	WHAT IS IT?	WHAT ARE THE BENEFITS?
PAX Voices	PAX Voices is the level of voice children should use during certain activities or in certain locations of the school. • **0-Inch Voice.** No talking. *Hand Signal:* Make a "0" with four fingers touching the thumb. • **3-Inch Voice.** Quiet conversational voice, barely louder than a whisper. *Hand Signal:* Hold three fingers in front of the mouth. • **3-Foot Voice.** Normal conversational voice but not so loud that the whole class can hear. *Hand Signal:* Hold hands several feet apart. • **10-Foot or Stage Voice.** Used when talking to the whole class. *Hand Signal:* Palm of hand extended out from body. • **30-Foot Voice.** Used only by adults in an emergency. **Adults will teach, praise, and recognize PAX Voices at school.**	• Improves children's ability to hear lessons. • Improves chances that children understand instructions. • Reduces noise and distractions. • Improves respect and calm. • Helps children with learning disabilities concentrate better.
Beat the Timer	• Beat the Timer is a powerful strategy to increase the accuracy and speed of task completion. • The teacher sets a timer for a short period of time and children attempt to complete a task before the timer goes off. **Adults will praise and recognize students for "beating the timer."**	• Less downtime or dawdling so that more instruction can happen. • Fewer disruptions. • Better accuracy. • Makes mundane tasks more fun. • Reduces arguments and stress.

©2003 by Hazelden Foundation. All rights reserved. Duplicating this page for personal or group use is permissible.

Home Link Flyer 2—page 3

CUE	WHAT IS IT?	WHAT ARE THE BENEFITS?
Stop Spleems and Go PAX signs	• Stop Spleems and Go PAX signs are placed on students' desks and on the walls. • Tapping on the signs allows the teacher to signal positive and negative behavior without interrupting learning activities. **Adults will praise and recognize students for obeying stop-and-go signs.**	• Reduces disruptions in classroom. • Keeps flow of instruction going smoothly. • More respectful for adults and students. • Keeps pace of instruction going for better learning.
PAX Stix	• PAX Stix are craft sticks with children's names on them. They are kept in a cup or the teacher's pocket. • The teacher randomly pulls out a stick and asks the child whose name appears on the stick to answer a question or to do a task.	• Increases participation and attention. • Decreases disruption. • Increases perceived fairness.

Home Link Flyer 3

PAX Tootle Notes Strategy

Dear Family,

During the next few weeks of playing the PAX Game, our classroom will start using PAX Tootle Notes. Tootles are the opposite of tattles. Tootling is looking for the positive actions of others, and telling them or others about the actions. Scientists have shown that tootles improve behavior, character, and social competence and reduce aggression or bullying in schools.*

We will be starting different kinds of tootles. Here are just some of the ways you may hear about tootles:

- *Peer Tootle Notes* involve young people giving notes to one another about positive behavior, or telling an adult about another student's positive behavior.

- *Teacher Home Tootles* are proven strategies to improve behavior at home and at school. I may send a Teacher Home Tootle about something good your child has done at school. If I do, I encourage you to praise your child for his or her positive behaviors.

- *Family Tootles* are a version that family members can write to one another. You can also send Family Tootles to school to let me know about something your child has done well at home.

In my classroom, we have lots to tootle about!

Sincerely,

---

* Alice S. Honig and Brad Pollack. (1988). *Effects of a Brief Intervention Program to Promote Prosocial Behaviors in Young Children.* ERIC_NO: ED316324. A. P. McCain and M. L. Kelley. (1993). Managing the classroom behavior of an ADHD preschooler: The efficacy of a school-home note intervention. *Child & Family Behavior Therapy,* 15, 33–44.

Home Link Flyer 4

My Wonderful PAX School

Dear Family,

Your child should have brought home a booklet called "My Wonderful PAX School" along with this letter.

Please plan to spend some time reading this booklet with your child. It tells you more about the PAX Game and how the game is benefiting your child, our classroom, and our school.

There are six brief chapters in the booklet. At the end of each chapter, there is a homework assignment. I am encouraging every child and family to read one chapter a day and to complete these assignments, which you can cut out of the booklet and send back to school with your child. Children will earn points for their team for returning the homework assignments on time.

The more families help reinforce what the children are learning in the PAX Game, the more our classroom will improve. I hope that home environments benefit, too.

Please start the booklet right away.

Sincerely,

Home Link Flyer 5

How Are Things Going with the PAX Game?

Dear Family,

Our PAX Game efforts are going very well. How do we know? We have been measuring how much the students' behavior has changed over time. We are so excited about this, we decided to send you a note to let you know what we are measuring and what our results have been.

Some of the things we are measuring include:

- Observing how much engaged learning there is in our classroom. The more students are fully engaged in learning, the better they will do.

- Observing declines in negative behavior or what we call Spleems. The less negative behavior in our classroom, the more time we have for teaching and learning. Learning to act positively will also positively impact children's futures.

- Counting how well and how fast children make transitions. The less time children spend in transitions, the fewer problem behaviors there are. Additionally, there is more time for real learning and fun.

- Reporting on how children feel the school has changed.

Here are some of the changes we have been seeing in our class/school, since we started playing the PAX Game:

_____

_____

_____

Thank you for your support of the PAX Game. It is really making a difference.

Sincerely,

APPENDIX C

"My Wonderful PAX School" Story

"My Wonderful PAX School" Story

This is an interactive story. Read it out loud to the children in a fun and engaging way, perhaps with a variety of voices. The goal of the story is to model the way in which the children should play the PAX Game and act as PAX Leaders.

Throughout the story there are Talk about It questions. Use these questions to check the children's understanding before you continue the story. *Optional:* Call on children to answer the questions using PAX Stix.

This story is a fictional account of some real events. The story is meant to make the listening children believe or pretend they are the real heroes in this story.

In addition to reading the story out loud, you may want to:

1. Show the appropriate PAX Game materials from this guide.
2. Tell the story using a feltboard and characters made from the illustrations in the Parent Booklet.
3. Have other adults or children read the story with different voices.
4. Tell the story using puppets made from paper plates, paper bags, or socks. Have the children help you create these puppets.
5. Have children act out the story as you tell it. Wear costumes to enhance the characters.

Time

Allow about thirty minutes to read the story. Then, have the class create a vision for a wonderful school as outlined on page 19 of this guide. Depending on the age or attention span of your students, you may want to take a break between reading the story and creating the vision.

Place

Make sure the place where you are reading is quiet enough for all to hear and participate, but allows you to move directly into creating a vision for a wonderful school.

The Story Begins . . .

I opened the door of my home and the grown-ups asked, "What happened at school today?"

"It was a terrible, awful, mean, and horrible day. The principal got mad because so many kids were bad. My teacher was sad because the class acted worse than yesterday. We learned nothing and had no fun. The day was very, very bad. I wish I had a magic tool to make a wonderful school, right away."

> **TALK ABOUT IT**
>
> **ASK:** Have any of you ever had a horrible day at school?
>
> **PROMPT:** Show me your hands if you want every day at school to be wonderful.

The grown-ups asked, "What would happen MORE at a wonderful school?"

"In a wonderful school I would . . . **See** more smiles, more kids learning, and people being kinder. **Hear** more nice words and laughter. **Feel** smarter, safer, and happier. **Do** more exciting work and learn more."

The grown-ups agreed, "That **does** sound like a wonderful school."

> **TALK ABOUT IT**
>
> **ASK:** What do you think would happen MORE at a wonderful school?
>
> **PROMPT:** Raise your hand if you want to go to a school where kids laugh and learn more, and have more fun.

Then, the grown-ups asked, "What would happen LESS at a wonderful school?"

The answers were easy. "In a wonderful school, I would . . . **See** fewer mean actions and interruptions. **Hear** fewer hurting words, less noise, and less yelling. **Feel** less worried, scared, mad, sad, or dumb. **Do** fewer things that hurt my school or class.

The grown-ups said, "All of this would make a wonderful school, too."

> **TALK ABOUT IT**
>
> **ASK:** What else would you see LESS of at a wonderful school?
>
> **PROMPT:** Raise your hands if you don't want people to yell or to be mean or hurt you at school.

The grown-ups said, "Perhaps you and your friends could invent something—maybe a game to make a wonderful school."

The next day, we talked to our teacher about making up a game. My teacher clapped with glee. "What a wonderful idea to make a wonderful school!"

We explained our ideas for how to play the game. "Will you have teams to play this game?" asked our teacher.

I said, "Yes, we will have several teams."

> **TALK ABOUT IT**
>
> **PROMPT:** Raise your hand if you would like to play a game to make a wonderful school.
>
> **ASK:** Why would teachers be happy if children came up with a game like this?

My teacher asked, "How are points scored in this game?"

I explained, "The whole class helps make up rules for a wonderful school. If a team member breaks one of these rules, it is a point *against* that child's team."

My teacher asked, "What is it called when somebody breaks a rule?"

My friend answered, "We call it a Spleem! A Spleem is something mean that hurts your team."

> **TALK ABOUT IT**
>
> **SAY:** Let's practice saying, "A Spleem is something mean that hurts my team." Have children repeat it several times.

The teacher asked, "How does a team win the game?"

"Oh," I explained. "It's simple to win. A team cannot score *more* than three Spleems during a game."

My teacher asked, "How long do we play the game?"

I answered, "When we first start the game, we play for only three to five minutes, but as we get better, we play for thirty to sixty minutes."

The teacher asked, "How do we keep track of the time?"

I said, "We use a timer!"

> **TALK ABOUT IT**
> **ASK:** If a team has four Spleems, does it win the game? (No)
> **ASK:** If a team had zero, one, two, or three Spleems, does it win? (Yes)

My friend said, "We use a scoreboard to keep track of the total number of games won and the total number of minutes won over the week. We call them PAX Wins and PAX Minutes."

(Optional: Hold up the PAX Wins Scoreboard for the children to see.)

I spoke up, "*PAX* means we are learning more, being happier, and being more peaceful. In the wonderful school, we will be healthier, too."

Another friend in the class added, "We thought the wonderful school would have lots of PAX. That's why we call it the PAX Game."

> **TALK ABOUT IT**
> **ASK:** What do we keep track of on the scoreboard? (PAX Wins and PAX Minutes)
> **ASK:** What is the game called? (The PAX Game)

Our teacher said, "We ought to have some prizes to celebrate when teams help make a wonderful school."

One kid in the class said, "My grandma lets us do silly things when we've been good for a day. We call them Granny's Wacky Prizes like these . . .

- make animal sounds for one minute,
- play hangman for a few minutes,
- make faces for one minute,
- jump in place for one minute,
- play tic-tac-toe for one minute,
- throw paper airplanes for two minutes."

Our teacher laughed. "Ho, ho, ho. Ha, ha, ha. These look fun. We could have three lists of prizes: teacher's list, Granny's Wacky Prizes, and a students' list."

TALK ABOUT IT

ASK: Which Granny's Wacky Prizes do you like?

The teacher asked, "Are there jobs or roles on the PAX Game teams?"

"Yes," I answered. "We have a bunch of positions on each team. They are . . .

(Optional: Hold up the PAX Game Job Cards.)

- PAX Captain cues the team when it is time to play the game, announces wins, and announces rewards for the team.
- PAX Coach helps team members do better at the game.
- PAX Tootler tootles on team members. Tootling is the opposite of tattling. It means telling on other kids who act in positive ways.
- PAX Go Getter gets papers and supplies for the team when asked to do so by the teacher.
- PAX Reminder tells the others to do their job if they forget that day."

> **TALK ABOUT IT**
>
> **ASK**: Who cues team members when it is time to play the PAX Game? (PAX Captain)
>
> **ASK**: Who helps other team members play the PAX Game better? (PAX Coach)
>
> **ASK**: What is tootling? (Telling others when someone does something positive)

Our teacher asked, "So how often should we play this game?"

A friend answered, "We should play three times a day. Then, the teacher should pick a secret time to play the game, too."

Our teacher asked, "Why should I do a secret game?"

I answered, "A secret game will help us learn faster, because it is a surprise. It will make us think more."

Our teacher liked our ideas for the PAX Game. "You know, I think we will start this game right away. I am going to make up a list of who will be on each team and a list of the prizes, and I will put up the scoreboards for the teams."

> **TALK ABOUT IT**
>
> **ASK**: How many times a day should the PAX Game be played? (Three times)

Soon, our teacher started playing the PAX Game with our class. My teacher first wrote down our ideas of a wonderful school or classroom on a big sheet of paper. Then my teacher explained the rules of the PAX Game.

(Optional: Read the following paragraph only to intermediate students.)

Our teacher asked what we should do if somebody keeps making Spleems, just to get attention. Our class decided that child would have to play on his or her own team until he or she won a game. Then, the child could rejoin the original team.

Finally, our class made a promise to become PAX Leaders, and we signed our names on the promise. We say that promise every day. We also have a PAX Leaders' motto: I better my world, and I better myself.

(Note: PAX Promise is optional.)

We played short PAX Games at first—three to five minutes at a time. When we made a Spleem, my teacher made a simple comment, "That was a Spleem," and marked the Spleem on the tally sheet. We learned not to say mean things if somebody got a Spleem, because that was a Spleem, too.

(Optional: Show the Spleems Tally Sheet and how you will tally Spleems.)

> **TALK ABOUT IT**
>
> **ASK:** What does the teacher do when you make a Spleem? (Makes a mark on the Spleems Tally Sheet)
>
> **ASK:** What happens if you make fun of someone who Spleems? (You get a Spleem for your team.)

Soon, we had won many PAX Games. We played longer games—as much as several hours in a day. Soon we had won hundreds of PAX Minutes. It was great! My teacher sent home special PAX Tootle Notes. They said things like, "Way to go for being a PAX Leader!"

> **TALK ABOUT IT**
>
> **ASK:** How would the adults in your home feel if you came home with a Tootle Note?

Soon, everyone heard about our PAX Game. Our principal heard about it. Our school board heard about it. The mayor of our city heard about it. The governor of our state heard about it. Even famous scientists came and learned about the PAX Game.

> **TALK ABOUT IT**
>
> **ASK:** Why do you think the PAX Game became so famous?

Productivity • Peace • Health • Happiness = PAX = Productivity • Peace • Health • Happiness

I am grown up now. The PAX Game is being played by millions of kids around the world. Scientists say that the PAX Game helps students learn more. They studied kids who played the game when they were little. The scientists studied the same kids again when they got older. Kids who played the game got into less trouble, they did fewer drugs, and they didn't hurt other people as much. They were happier, too.

People often ask me why we invented the game. And my answer is always the same. It was because:

(Allow a few students to complete the sentence.)

All we wanted to do was create a wonderful school, but we ended up creating a wonderful world, too. Maybe you can do the same. After all, you're a PAX Leader, too!

APPENDIX D

Meeting Federal, State, and Other Mandates

Meeting Federal, State, and Other Mandates

Each year, the burden on schools seems to grow with a variety of initiatives: No Child Left Behind Act, Individuals with Disabilities Education Act (special education), Section 504, Safe and Drug-Free Schools Act, character education, and migrant children education. Fortunately, the *PAX Good Behavior Game* fulfills these diverse mandates, as briefly summarized in the following chart.

MANDATE	HOW THE PAX GAME HELPS
No Child Left Behind Act	• The PAX Game is a research-based set of practices that increases time for fully engaged learning and academics. • The powerful effects of the PAX Game reduce the likelihood that a school will be labeled as persistently dangerous. • The PAX Game provides improved conditions for increasing academic performance of disadvantaged students.
Safe and Drug-Free Schools	• Strong scientific and long-term evidence indicates that the PAX Game reduces substance use and aggression in students. • The PAX Game is named a best practice in this area.
Individuals with Disabilities Education Act (IDEA)	• The IDEA stipulates that, to the extent possible, children with disabilities be educated in regular classes with their nondisabled peers with appropriate supplementary aids and services. The PAX Game helps special-needs children participate more fully in the regular classroom. • The PAX Game can be used as part of a Functional Behavioral Assessment and Positive Behavioral Intervention Plan as required by law.
Section 504 of the Rehabilitation Act of 1973	• The Office of Civil Rights clarifies that schools must evaluate children for special education who are suspected of having attention deficit disorder based on parental request. • The PAX Game aids in reducing the symptoms of attention deficit–hyperactivity disorder/attention deficit disorder.

Mandates—page 2

MANDATE	HOW THE PAX GAME HELPS
School improvement plans	• The PAX Game results in school improvement that can be documented by valid measures such as teacher ratings of student behavior, student ratings of self and peers, and direct observation of engaged instruction (a key predictor of standardized achievement).
Civil rights issues	• The PAX Game reduces the serious and minor discipline problems that have historically led to the over-representation of minority children or youth as dropouts or in special education. • The PAX Game and related interventions reduce victimization of *all* children that can lead to legal challenges.
Tobacco prevention	• The PAX Game, used in elementary school, profoundly reduces the risk of tobacco use in adolescence by addressing key risk and protective factors.
School reform	• Comprehensive reforms must be grounded in scientifically based research and effective practice. The PAX Game components meet all those criteria, with effect sizes that run between +.4 and +.7. • The PAX Game can be combined with other research-based interventions such as classwide peer tutoring or academic improvement strategies to meet requirements of school reform.
Character education	• The PAX Game and related tools provide a language of character development related to trust, helpfulness, respect, promise keeping, and caring.
School safety and discipline plans	• The PAX Game and related research-based strategies have been shown to reduce all of the behaviors that endanger school safety. • The PAX Game and related research-based strategies can reduce referrals, suspensions, and expulsions substantially, which is the goal of a discipline plan.

MANDATE	HOW THE PAX GAME HELPS
Resiliency initiatives	• Based on published studies, the PAX Game addresses resiliency factors such as the following: 1. clear and consistent boundaries 2. reduced threats and increased bonding 3. high expectations 4. increased caring and support 5. meaningful roles 6. social skills
Mental health services	• The PAX Game has replicated scientific results in reducing symptoms of attention deficit–hyperactivity disorder, oppositional defiant disorder, conduct disorders, developmental disorders, and spectrum disorders, as outlined by the American Psychiatric Association. • The PAX Game may reduce symptoms of depression, post-traumatic stress disorder, and anxiety disorders.

APPENDIX E

PAX Good Behavior Game Evaluation Tools

PAX Yesterday Survey, 137

Spleems Observation Form, 139

Planned Activity Check, 141

PAX Yesterday Survey

My teacher is: _____

My school is: _____

Today's date is: _____

DO NOT PUT YOUR NAME ON THIS SURVEY

Think about the good things and bad things that happened yesterday in our classroom. Read or listen to each question below. Then mark an **X** if something never happened, happened a little, or happened a lot.

Here is an example:

| My teacher talked to us. | never | a little | a ~~lot~~ ✗ |

1. Other kids were mean to me.	never	a little	a lot
2. Other kids made it hard for me to learn in class.	never	a little	a lot
3. I paid attention to the teacher.	never	a little	a lot
4. I worked hard at learning.	never	a little	a lot
5. I squirmed and fidgeted.	never	a little	a lot
6. I did what the teacher asked quickly.	never	a little	a lot
7. Other kids thanked me for helping them.	never	a little	a lot
8. Other kids or adults were mad, sad, or angry.	never	a little	a lot
9. Adults noticed I did something good.	never	a little	a lot
10. I thanked another kid for helping me or being nice.	never	a little	a lot

©2003 by Hazelden Foundation. All rights reserved. Duplicating this page for personal or group use is permissible.

Spleems Observation Form

Classroom _____   Date _____   Observer _____

Brief Description of Activity _____

Instructions

Observe students every minute for fifteen minutes. During each minute, tally the number of Spleems that occur and the activity being done on the form below. After fifteen minutes, complete the rest of the form and graph the results.

STUDENT/GROUPS	ONE-MINUTE INTERVALS														
	1	2	3	4	5	6	7	8	9	10	11	12	13	14	15
Number of children in room															
Tally of disruptions by interval (hash /// marks)															
Total number by interval															
A. Total number of disruptions per 15 minutes															
B. Divide total disruptions (A) by average number of children in room.															
C. Multiply B by 4 to express rate of disruptions per hour per student. Graph data.															
Below, check off types of activities done during interval:															
Transition (line up, change places)															
Activity maintenance (paper passed, etc.)															
Teacher lecture															
Individual seatwork															
Group or whole class discussion															
Peer teaching															
Reading or writing															
Math or science															
Other academic:															
Non-academic:															
Teacher disciplined child or classroom															
Other:															

Planned Activity Check

Classroom _____   Date _____   Observer _____

Brief Description of Activity _____

Instructions

Observe students every minute for fifteen minutes. For each minute, tally the number of children in the room, the number engaged in learning, the percentage engaged in learning, and the activity being done on the form below. After fifteen minutes, calculate the average percent of children engaged in learning and graph the results.

STUDENT/GROUPS	ONE-MINUTE INTERVALS														
	1	2	3	4	5	6	7	8	9	10	11	12	13	14	15
Number of children in room															
Number engaged in learning															
Percent engaged in learning															
AVERAGE percent engaged during observation (Graph data)															
Below, check off types of activities done during interval:															
Transition (line up, change places)															
Activity maintenance (paper passed, etc.)															
Teacher lecture															
Individual seatwork															
Group or whole class discussion															
Peer teaching															
Reading or writing															
Math or science															
Other academic:															
Non-academic:															
Teacher disciplined child or classroom															
Other:															

©2003 by Hazelden Foundation. All rights reserved. Duplicating this page for personal or group use is permissible.

NOTES

1. M. J. Koepp et al. (1998). Evidence for striatal dopamine release during a video game. *Nature,* 393 (6682), 266–68.

2. N. S. Ialongo et al. (1999). Proximal impact of two first-grade preventive interventions on the early risk behaviors for later substance abuse, depression, and antisocial behavior. *American Journal of Community Psychology,* 27 (5), 599–641.

3. D. C. Guevremont, P. G. Osnes, and T. F. Stokes. (1986). Programming maintenance after correspondence training interventions with children. *Journal of Applied Behavior Analysis,* 19, 215–19. V. Anderson and F. Merrett. (1997). The use of correspondence training in improving the in-class behaviour of very troublesome secondary school children. *Educational Psychology,* 17, 313–28. R. A. Baer. (1990). Correspondence training: Review and current issues. *Research in Developmental Disabilities,* 11, 379–93. T. Glynn, F. Merrett, and S. Houghton. (1991). Reducing troublesome behaviour in three secondary pupils through correspondence training. *Educational Studies,* 17, 273–83. J. Merrett and F. Merrett. (1997). Correspondence training as a means of improving study skills. *Educational Psychology,* 17, 469–82. F. A. Paniagua. (1992). Verbal-nonverbal correspondence training with ADHD children. *Behavior Modification,* 16, 226–52. F. A. Paniagua and S. A. Black. (1990). Management and prevention of hyperactivity and conduct disorders in 8–10 year old boys through correspondence training procedures. *Child & Family Behavior Therapy,* 12, 23–56. F. A. Paniagua and S. A. Black. (1992). Correspondence training and observational learning in the management of hyperactive children: A preliminary study. *Child & Family Behavior Therapy,* 14, 1–19. F. A. Paniagua, P. B. Morrison, and S. A. Black. (1990). Management of a hyperactive-conduct disordered child through correspondence training: A preliminary study. *Journal of Behavior Therapy & Experimental Psychiatry,* 21, 63–68. J. V. Roca and A. M. Gross. (1996). Report-do-report: Promoting setting and setting-time generalization. *Education & Treatment of Children,* 19, 408–24. J. M. Weninger and R.A. Baer. (1990). Correspondence training with time delay: A comparison with reinforcement of compliance. *Education & Treatment of Children,* 13, 36–44. J. A. Williams and T. F. Stokes. (1982). Some parameters of correspondence training and generalized verbal control. *Child & Family Behavior Therapy,* 4, 11–32.

4. K. L. Altman and T.E. Linton. (1971). Operant conditioning in the classroom setting: A review of the research. *Journal of Educational Research,* 64, 277–86. C. D. Broussard and J. Northup. (1995). An approach to functional assessment and analysis of disruptive behavior in regular education classrooms. *School Psychology Quarterly,* 10, 151–64. C. Broussard and J. Northup. (1997). The use of functional analysis to

develop peer interventions for disruptive classroom behavior. *School Psychology Quarterly,* 12, 65–76. W. A. Flood et al. (2002). Peer-mediated reinforcement plus prompting as treatment for off-task behavior in children with attention deficit–hyperactivity disorder. *Journal of Applied Behavior Analysis,* 35, 199–204. K. M. Jones, H. A. Drew, and N. L. Weber. (2000). Noncontingent peer attention as treatment for disruptive classroom behavior. *Journal of Applied Behavior Analysis,* 33, 343–46. T. J. Lewis and G. Sugai. (1996). Descriptive and experimental analysis of teacher and peer attention and the use of assessment-based intervention to improve pro-social behavior. *Journal of Behavioral Education,* 6, 7–24. T. J. Lewis and G. Sugai. (1996). Functional assessment of problem behavior: A pilot investigation on the comparative and interactive effects of teacher and peer social attention on students in general education settings. *School Psychology Quarterly,* 11, 1–19. B. A. Marcus et al. (2001). An experimental analysis of aggression. *Behavior Modification,* 25, 189–213. J. Northrup et al. (1997). A preliminary analysis of interactive effects between common classroom contingencies and methylphenidate. *Journal of Applied Behavior Analysis,* 30, 121–45. J. Northup et al. (1995). The differential effects of teacher and peer attention on the disruptive classroom behavior of three children with a diagnosis of attention deficit–hyperactivity disorder. *Journal of Applied Behavior Analysis,* 28, 227–28. J. T. Simmons and B. H. Wasik. (1976). Grouping strategies, peer influence, and free time as classroom management techniques with first- and third-grade children. *Journal of School Psychology,* 14, 322–32.

5. V. W. Harris and J. A. Sherman. (1973). Use and analysis of the "Good Behavior Game" to reduce disruptive classroom behavior. *Journal of Applied Behavior Analysis,* 6, 405–17.

6. V. Anderson and F. Merrett. (1997). The use of correspondence training in improving the in-class behaviour of very troublesome secondary school children. *Educational Psychology,* 17, 313–28. R. A. Baer. (1990). Correspondence training: Review and current issues. *Research in Developmental Disabilities,* 11, 379–93. T. Glynn, F. Merrett, and S. Houghton. (1991). Reducing troublesome behaviour in three secondary pupils through correspondence training. *Educational Studies,* 17, 273–83. J. Merrett and F. Merrett. (1997). Correspondence training as a means of improving study skills. *Educational Psychology,* 17, 469–82. F. A. Paniagua. (1992). Verbal-nonverbal correspondence training with ADHD children. *Behavior Modification,* 16, 226–52. F. A. Paniagua and S. A. Black. (1990). Management and prevention of hyperactivity and conduct disorders in 8-10 year old boys through correspondence training procedures. *Child & Family Behavior Therapy,* 12, 23–56. F. A. Paniagua and S. A. Black. (1992). Correspondence training and observational learning in the management of hyperactive children: A preliminary study. *Child & Family Behavior Therapy,* 14, 1–19. F. A. Paniagua, P. B. Morrison, and S. A. Black. (1990). Management of a hyperactive-conduct disordered child through correspondence training: A preliminary study. *Journal of Behavior Therapy & Experimental Psychiatry,* 21, 63–68. J. V. Roca and A. M. Gross. (1996). Report-do-report: Promoting setting and setting-time

generalization. *Education & Treatment of Children,* 19, 408–24. J. M. Weninger and R. A. Baer. (1990). Correspondence training with time delay: A comparison with reinforcement of compliance. *Education & Treatment of Children,* 13, 36–44. J. A. Williams and T. F. Stokes. (1982). Some parameters of correspondence training and generalized verbal control. *Child & Family Behavior Therapy,* 4, 11–32.

7. B. Rogoff et al. (1975). Age of assignment of roles and responsibilities to children: A cross-cultural survey. *Human Development,* 18, 353–69.

8. T. M. Flynn. (1991). Development of social, personal and cognitive skills of preschool children in Montessori and traditional preschool programs. *Early Child Development & Care,* 72, 117–24. L. B. Miller and R. P. Bizzell. (1983). Long-term effects of four preschool programs: Sixth, seventh, and eighth grades. *Child Development,* 54, 727–41. L. B. Miller and R. P. Bizzell. (1984). Long-term effects of four preschool programs: Ninth- and tenth-grade results. *Child Development,* 55, 1570–87. C. Greenwood. (1997). Classwide peer tutoring. *Behavior & Social Issues,* 7, 53–57. C. Greenwood et al. (1993). Achievement, placement, and services: Middle school benefits of Classwide Peer Tutoring used at the elementary school. *School Psychology Review,* 22, 497–516. C. R. Greenwood, J. C. Delquadri, and R. V. Hall. (1989). Longitudinal effects of classwide peer tutoring. *Journal of Educational Psychology,* 81, 371–83.

9. D. C. Simmons et al. (1994). Importance of instructional complexity and role reciprocity to classwide peer tutoring. *Learning Disabilities Research & Practice,* 9, 203–12.

10. S. E. Rosenkoetter and S. A. Fowler. (1986). Teaching mainstreamed children to manage daily transitions. *Teaching Exceptional Children,* 19, 20–23. L. A. Doke and T. R. Risley. (1972). The organization of day-care environments: Required vs. optional activities. *Journal of Applied Behavior Analysis,* 5 (4), 405–20. P. J. Krantz and T. Risley. (1977). Behavioral ecology in the classroom. In K. D. O'Leary and S. G. O'Leary (Eds.), *Classroom management: The successful use of behavior modification,* 2nd ed., 349–66. New York: Pergamon Press.

11. L. W. Nober. (1973). Auditory discrimination and classroom noise. *Reading Teacher,* 27, 288–91. G. W. Schmidt and R. E. Ulrich. (1969). Effects of group contingent events upon classroom noise. *Journal of Applied Behavior Analysis,* 2, 171–79. G. Larson and B. Petersen. (1978). Does noise limit the learning of young listeners? *Elementary School Journal,* 78, 264–65.

12. R. A. Astor, H. A. Meyer, and R. O. Pitner. (2001). Elementary and middle school students' perceptions of violence-prone school subcontexts. *Elementary School Journal,* 101, 511–28.

13. A. Hilton. (1985). A positive approach to classroom behavior problems. *Academic Therapy,* 20, 469–73.

14. This story is based on the procedures and implementation of several published studies: G. R. Mayer et al. (1983). Preventing school vandalism and improving discipline: A three-year study. *Journal of Applied Behavior Analysis,* 16, 355–69. T. H. Cashwell, C. H. Skinner, and E. S. Smith. (2001). Increasing second-grade students' reports of peers' prosocial behaviors via direct instruction, group reinforcement, and progress feedback: A replication and extension. *Education & Treatment of Children,* 24, 161–75. C. H. Skinner, T. H. Cashwell, and A. L. Skinner. (2000). Increasing tootling: The effects of a peer-monitored group contingency program on students' reports of peers' prosocial behaviors. *Psychology in the Schools,* 37, 263–27.

15. A. P. McCain and M. L. Kelley. (1993). Managing the classroom behavior of an ADHD preschooler: The efficacy of a school-home note intervention. *Child & Family Behavior Therapy,* 15, 33–44.

16. A. U. Rickel and R. B. Fields. (1983). Storybook models and achievement behavior of preschool children. *Psychology in the Schools,* 20, 105–13. L. Z. McArthur and S. V. Eisen. (1976). Achievements of male and female storybook characters as determinants of achievement behavior by boys and girls. *Journal of Personality & Social Psychology,* 33, 467–73. W. L. Mikulas et al. (1985). Behavioral bibliotherapy and games for treating fear of the dark. *Child & Family Behavior Therapy,* 7, 1–7. Z. Shechtman and M. Ben-David. (1999). Individual and group psychotherapy of childhood aggression: A comparison of outcomes and processes. *Group Dynamics,* 3, 263–74. Z. Shechtman. (1999). Bibliotherapy: An indirect approach to treatment of childhood aggression. *Child Psychiatry & Human Development,* 30, 39–53. G. Mettetal. (1996). Non-clinical interventions for families with temperamentally difficult children. *Early Child Development & Care,* 121, 119–33. S. Hunt and M. Adams. (1989). Bibliotherapy-based Dry Bed Training: A pilot study. *Behavioural Psychotherapy,* 17, 290–301. T. R. Shepherd and J. Koberstein. (1989). Books, puppets, and sharing: Teaching preschool children to share. *Psychology in the Schools,* 26, 311–16. L. J. Cohen. (1987). Bibliotherapy: Using literature to help children deal with difficult problems. *Journal of Psychosocial Nursing & Mental Health Services,* 25, 20–24.

17. V. Crane and B. L. Ballif. (1973). Effects of adult modeling and rule structure on responses to moral situations of children in fifth-grade classrooms. *Journal of Experimental Education,* 41, 49–52. F. Li, W. Ye, and L. Chen. (1994). Effects of the training of transference on young children's sharing behavior. *Psychological Science (China),* 17, 150–54. Y. Israely and J. Guttmann. (1983). Children's sharing behavior as a function of exposure to puppet-show and story models. *Journal of Genetic Psychology,* 142, 311–12. M. K. Alvord and K. D. O'Leary. (1985). Teaching children to share through stories. *Psychology in the Schools,* 22, 323–30. L. Greene et al. (1999). Home-based consultation for parents of young children with behavioral problems. *Child & Family Behavior Therapy,* 21, 19–45. M. R. Sanders. (1982). The effects of instructions, feedback, and cueing procedures in behavioural parent training. *Australian Journal of Psychology,* 34, 53–69.

18. D. D. Embry et al. (1996). PeaceBuilders: A theoretically driven, school-based model for early violence prevention. *American Journal of Preventive Medicine,* 12, 91–100.

19. D. V. Ary, L. James, and A. Biglan. (1999). Parent-daughter discussions to discourage tobacco use: Feasibility and content. *Adolescence,* 34, 275–82. T. K. Taylor and A. Biglan. (1998). Behavioral family interventions for improving child-rearing: A review of the literature for clinicians and policy makers. *Clinical Child & Family Psychology Review,* 1, 41–60. H. B. Clark et al. (1977). A parent advice package for family shopping trips: Development and evaluation. *Journal of Applied Behavior Analysis,* 10, 605–24.

20. R. Goodman and S. Scott. (1999). Comparing the Strengths and Difficulties Questionnaire and the Child Behavior Checklist: Is small beautiful? *Journal of Abnormal Child Psychology,* 27, 17–24.

NOTES

NOTES

NOTES

Hazelden, a national nonprofit organization founded in 1949, helps people reclaim their lives from the disease of addiction. Built on decades of knowledge and experience, Hazelden offers a comprehensive approach to addiction that addresses the full range of patient, family, and professional needs, including treatment and continuing care for youth and adults, research, higher learning, public education and advocacy, and publishing.

A life of recovery is lived "one day at a time." Hazelden publications, both educational and inspirational, support and strengthen lifelong recovery. In 1954, Hazelden published *Twenty-Four Hours a Day*, the first daily meditation book for recovering alcoholics, and Hazelden continues to publish works to inspire and guide individuals in treatment and recovery, and their loved ones. Professionals who work to prevent and treat addiction also turn to Hazelden for evidence-based curricula, informational materials, and videos for use in schools, treatment programs, and correctional programs.

Through published works, Hazelden extends the reach of hope, encouragement, help, and support to individuals, families, and communities affected by addiction and related issues.

For questions about Hazelden publications,
please call **800-328-9000** or visit us online at **hazelden.org/bookstore**.

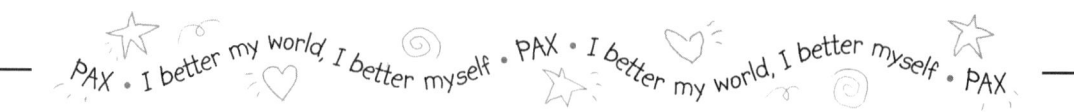

Thank you for purchasing the *PAX Good Behavior Game.*

Restock or enhance your game with these components:

- **Schoolwide Implementation Guide**
  This manual shows how to make your school a PAX school. It gets all site leaders onboard—staff, student representatives, families, and community stakeholders—for easy implementation of this best practices and research-based game. *Order No. 2117*

- **Video**
  An excellent tool to help teachers implement the *PAX Good Behavior Game. Order No. 7358*

- **Home Notes**
  Colorful, mailable postcards get parents interested and involved in the PAX Game while letting them know about their child's positive behavior. Sold in packs of 120 (4 designs, 30 of each design). *Order No. 2124*

- **Reward stickers**
  Make sure you have plenty on hand! Refill orders available in quantities of 60 (10 of each design). *Order No. 2125*

- **Team Wristbands**
  A fun, easy way to reinforce team spirit and belonging. Sturdy acrylic with snap closure. Pack includes 32 wristbands in 4 colors, 8 wristbands in each color. *Order No. 2126*

- **Training**
  Ideal for schoolwide or multiclass implementation, these training seminars show site leaders how to play the game and how to adapt it to their specific site needs. On-site or regional seminars available.

To place an order or for training information, call us today at 1-800-328-9000. Or visit our Web site at www.hazelden.org/bookplace.